MONSTER TRUCK MADNESS

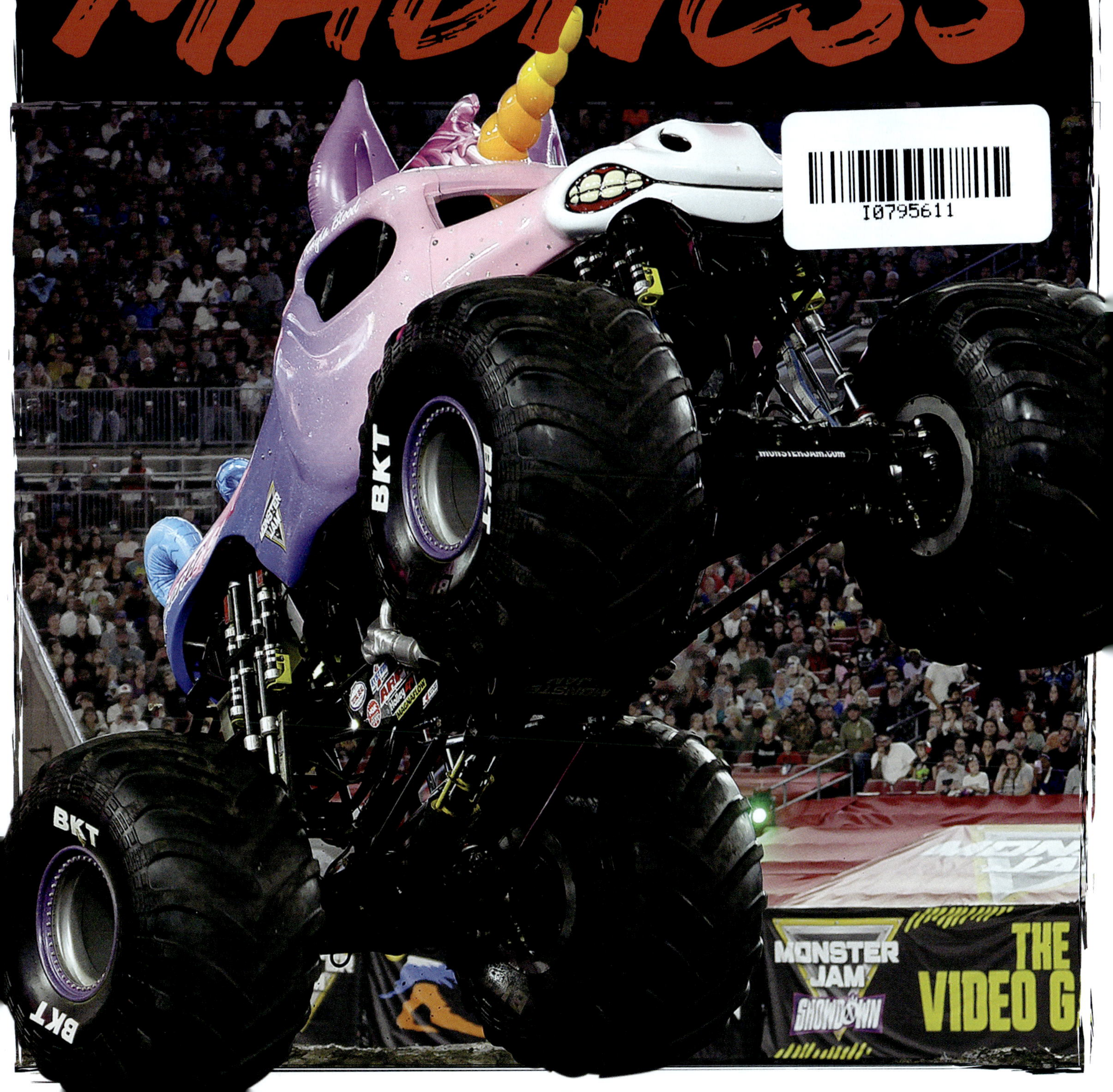

This book is available in quantity at special discounts for your group or organization.

For further information, contact:

Triumph Books LLC
814 North Franklin Street
Chicago, Illinois 60610

Phone: (312) 337-0747
www.triumphbooks.com

Printed in U.S.A.
ISBN: 979-8-89855-017-2

Content packaged by Mojo Media, Inc.
Joe Funk: Editor
Jason Hinman: Creative Director
Don Gulbrandsen: Copy Editor

All photos by Andrew Fielder unless otherwise indicated.

MONSTER TRUCK MADNESS

CONTENTS

MONSTER TRUCK MADNESS

INTRODUCTION

Big engines. Mega tires. Gigantic attitudes. Welcome to the high-octane, mud-slinging, suspension-shattering world of monster trucks, a place where subtlety goes to die, gravity is suspended, and horsepower is measured in "are you serious right now?"

This is a world built on excess, including chromoly steel, internal combustion, heavy fuel, fan interaction, and rides on tires taller than most cars. Monster trucks aren't just vehicles, they're mechanical exclamation points, engineered to shout over roaring crowds and rattling grandstands.

At first glance, they appear almost cartoonish: a familiar pickup truck stretched, lifted, and transformed into something towering and unapologetically absurd. But look closer, and the spectacle sharpens into precision. Beneath the fiberglass shells and outrageous paint jobs lies a purpose-built lattice of steel; rugged machines designed to endure impacts that would reduce ordinary vehicles to scrap.

But machines like these don't become legends on engineering alone. They need drivers, a rare breed of individuals who look at a 10,000-pound vehicle and think, "Yes, I shall flip this, or tip it on two tires." Enter icons like Dennis Anderson, the creator of the legendary Grave Digger, whose name became synonymous with the sport itself. Or Tom Meents, one of the most decorated drivers in history, known for pushing both himself and his truck beyond what seemed mechanically or logically possible. And then there's Adam Anderson, carrying on a family legacy while redefining what modern monster truck driving can be.

What makes monster trucks truly remarkable isn't just their size or spectacle, it's their resilience. These machines are built to fail spectacularly and keep going anyway. Axles twist, shocks compress, and frames flex, but still they charge forward, mud flying and engines roaring, as if "enough" was never part of the design brief.

This book is your backstage pass plus a front row seat to the that world: the machines, the mayhem, and the mavericks behind it all. It's about how a simple idea–make a truck bigger and badder– has evolved into a global phenomenon of controlled destruction and engineered insanity that has smashed its way into a distinctly American creation of calamitous culture.

TOM MEENTS
9 TIME WORLD
CHAMPION
NGK

THE TRU

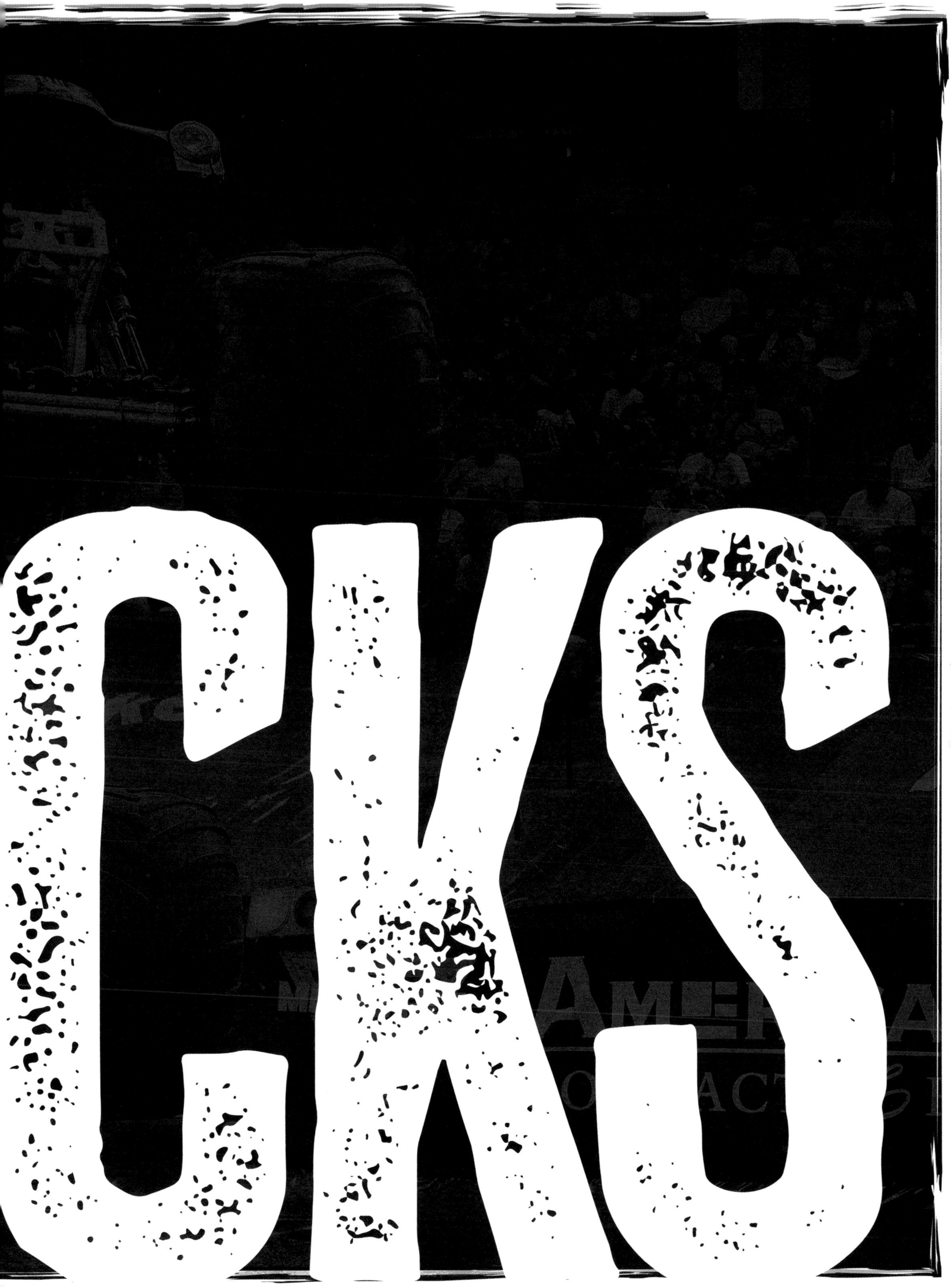
CKS

GRAVE DIGGER

Grave Digger is one of the most iconic and recognizable vehicles in motorsports history, particularly within the world of monster trucks. Since its creation in the early 1980s, it has evolved from a homemade mud bogging truck into a global entertainment phenomenon closely associated with the sport of monster truck racing and freestyle performance.

1982

YEAR DENNIS ANDERSON BUILT THE VERY FIRST GRAVE DIGGER.

"I'LL TAKE THIS OLD JUNK AND DIG YOU A GRAVE WITH IT."
— DENNIS ANDERSON

FOR 30 YEARS
30TH ANNIVERSARY
GRAVE DIGGER
section 134

ORIGINS AND CREATION

Grave Digger was created in 1982 by Dennis Anderson in North Carolina. Originally, it was not intended to be a monster truck at all, but rather a mud bogging vehicle built from inexpensive, salvaged parts. The first version used a 1950s-era Ford pickup body and was assembled on a tight budget, reflecting Anderson's resourcefulness and mechanical skill.

The name "Grave Digger" came from a remark Anderson made to competitors who mocked his rough-looking truck. He famously said he would "take this old junk and dig you a grave with it," a line that became part of motorsports lore.

TRANSITION TO MONSTER TRUCKS

Grave Digger's transformation into a monster truck happened somewhat by accident. At one event, a scheduled monster truck failed to appear, and Anderson stepped in with his modified mud truck, now equipped with larger tires, to crush cars for the crowd. The performance was a hit, and it marked the beginning of Grave Digger's legend in monster trucks.

40+ YEARS

HOW LONG GRAVE DIGGER HAS BEEN ACTIVE IN MOTORSPORTS.

GRAVE DIGGER HELPED POPULARIZE FREESTYLE COMPETITION IN MONSTER JAM, WHERE WILD TRICKS MATTER AS MUCH AS RACING.

BKT
BKT
metro
by T-Mobile

By the mid-1980s, the souped-up truck had been rebuilt into a full-fledged monster truck with massive tires, a reinforced chassis, and a more powerful engine. Around this time, it adopted its now-famous black paint scheme featuring green flames, graveyard imagery, and glowing red headlights–visual elements that helped define its spooky, rebellious identity.

RISE TO FAME

During the late 1980s and early 1990s, Grave Digger ascended to become one of the most popular monster trucks in the United States. Anderson's aggressive, all-or-nothing driving style characterized by huge jumps, hard landings, and frequent crashes made the truck a fan favorite.

A major breakthrough came when Grave Digger defeated its biggest rival, BIGFOOT, in a televised event in 1987. This victory helped elevate the truck's national profile and cemented its reputation as a top competitor.

As the sport grew, Grave Digger became a central attraction in events organized by the United States Hot Rod Association and later in the Monster Jam series. Its popularity led to the creation of multiple Grave Digger trucks, allowing the brand to appear at several events simultaneously.

ITS BLACK-AND-GREEN GRAVEYARD THEME, PAIRED WITH THE SONG "BAD TO THE BONE," MADE IT THE MOST RECOGNIZABLE MONSTER TRUCK IN THE WORLD.

EXPANSION INTO A FRANCHISE

As Grave Digger's popularity grew, it evolved into a full-fledged franchise rather than a single vehicle. Over the decades, dozens of trucks have carried the Grave Digger name, each with its own number and driver.

In 1998, Anderson sold the team to what is now known as Feld Entertainment, the organization behind Monster Jam. Despite the sale, Anderson remained heavily involved as a driver and mentor for many years.

Today, multiple drivers including members of Anderson's own family, continue to operate Grave Digger trucks, keeping the legacy alive for new generations of fans.

CULTURAL IMPACT

Grave Digger is widely considered the most famous monster truck of all time. Its distinctive appearance, dramatic performances, and long history have made it a symbol of the sport itself. For many fans, a monster truck show isn't the same without its presence.

The truck's influence extends beyond live events. It has appeared in video games, toys, television shows, and merchandise, becoming a staple of pop culture associated with motorsports entertainment.

GRAVE DIGGER
BKT
BKT

Its signature theme song, "Bad to the Bone," along with its graveyard-themed imagery, has further reinforced its identity as a rebellious and larger-than-life character within the sport.

LEGACY

Grave Digger has remained active for over four decades, an impressive lifespan in a sport known for constant evolution and mechanical wear. Even after Dennis Anderson's retirement from driving in 2017, the truck continues to compete and headline events worldwide.

Its legacy lies not only in its competitive success such as multiple championship wins, but also in its role in shaping monster truck culture. From pioneering freestyle performances to inspiring future drivers, Grave Digger has helped define what a monster truck is and what it represents.

From a scrapyard-built mud truck to a global icon, Grave Digger's story is one of innovation, perseverance, and showmanship. Its blend of engineering, spectacle, and personality has made it a cornerstone of motorsports entertainment. More than just a vehicle, Grave Digger is a symbol of the excitement and creativity that defines monster truck culture, and it continues to impress the living daylights out of audiences around the world.

GRAVE DIGGER
BKT
ARP
MAGNAFLOW

BKT
GRAVE DIGGER
BAD TO THE BONE
DIGGER

THE ORIGINAL GRAVE DIGGER WAS BUILT IN 1982 BY DENNIS ANDERSON USING JUNKYARD PARTS AND AN OLD PICKUP BODY.

EL TORO LOCO

Underneath the body, El Toro Loco shares the same fundamental engineering as most top-tier monster trucks. Despite weighing roughly 10,000 pounds, El Toro Loco can accelerate quickly and perform complex maneuvers thanks to its high power-to-weight ratio and specialized suspension system.

2001

FIRST DEBUTED IN MONSTER JAM.

BKT
EL TORO LOCO
MONSTER JAM
BKT

WILD STYLE

What truly defines El Toro Loco, however, is its driving style. The truck is known for its unpredictability and willingness to push limits, often attempting daring stunts that risk rollovers or mechanical failure. This high-risk approach has led to some of the most memorable moments in Monster Jam history, including spectacular crashes and near-impossible saves. Fans expect El Toro Loco to deliver excitement, whether that means it's snorting sound effects and smoke coming from its horns, to soaring over obstacles in racing competitions, or performing chaotic and crowd-thrilling tricks during freestyle runs.

DARING DRIVERS

Over the years, multiple drivers have taken the wheel of El Toro Loco, each bringing their own personality and flair. Notable drivers include Lupe Soza, one of the original and most closely associated drivers with the truck, as well as Mark List and Armando Castro. Each driver has contributed to the truck's legacy, adapting its aggressive persona while adding unique driving techniques and showmanship.

SPECS

HORSEPOWER: ~1,500 HP SUPERCHARGED V8 ENGINE

WEIGHT: ~12,000 POUNDS (ABOUT 5,400 KG)

TOP SPEED: 100 MPH (160 KM/H) IN OPTIMAL CONDITIONS

2 MINUTES: TYPICAL FREESTYLE RUN TIME

A LITERAL BULLPEN

El Toro Loco competes in several types of events within Monster Jam. In racing, trucks go head-to-head on short, obstacle-filled tracks, where speed and precision are key. In freestyle competitions, drivers have a set amount of time, usually around two minutes, to perform tricks, jumps, and stunts, and are judged on creativity, difficulty, and execution. It is in freestyle where El Toro Loco often shines brightest, embracing its "crazy bull" identity with wild, unpredictable performances that can either earn top scores or end in dramatic wrecks.

The truck has also been part of various spin-offs and themed versions over the years. These include special paint schemes and even alternative versions like "El Toro Loco Ice" and "El Toro Loco Fire," which are part of Monster Jam's elemental series. These variants maintain the core bull identity while adding new visual themes and slight performance tweaks, keeping the brand fresh and engaging for repeat audiences.

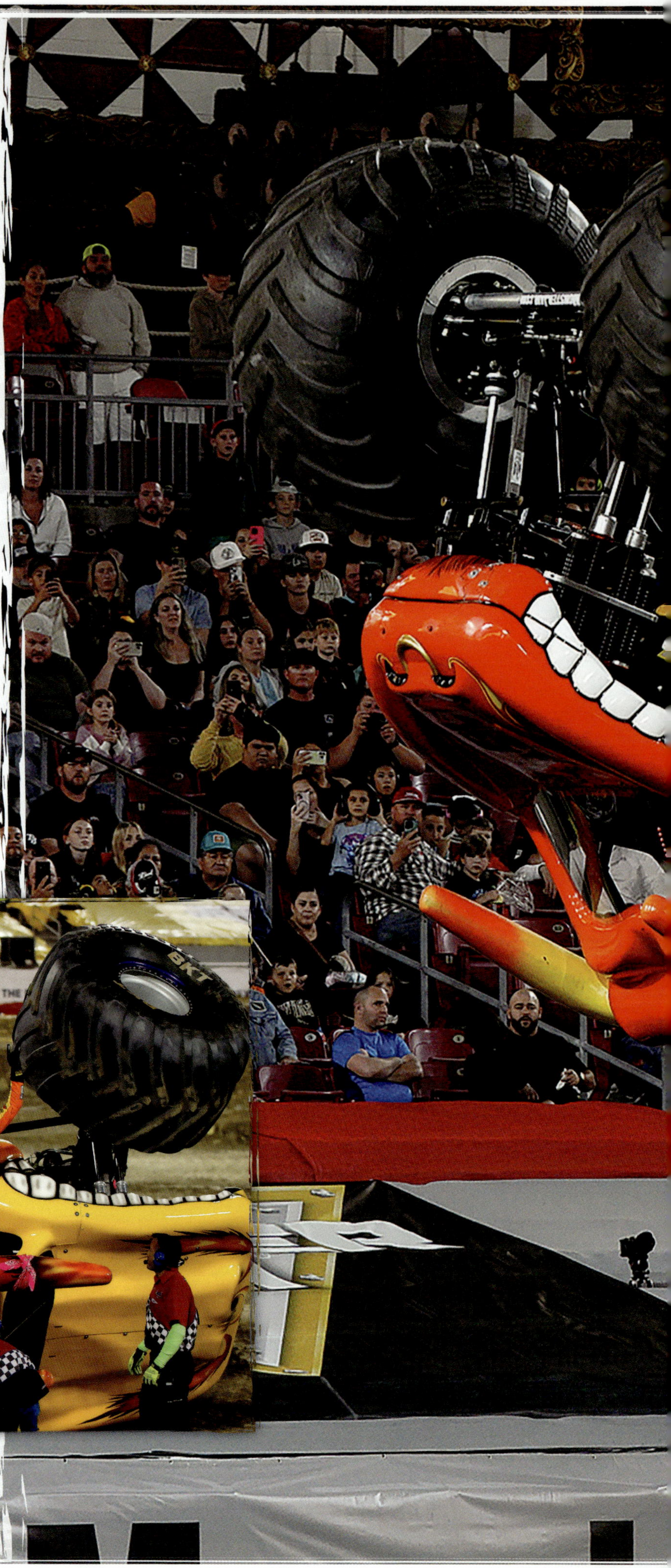

BUCCANEERS
BKT
El Toro Loco
MONSTER JAM

CULTURAL IDENTITY

Culturally, El Toro Loco plays an important role in the broader appeal of monster truck events. It represents the theatrical side of the sport, where vehicles are not just machines but characters. This approach helps bridge the gap between motorsport and entertainment, making Monster Jam events feel closer to a live-action spectacle than a traditional race. Kids often wear El Toro Loco merchandise, including horned hats and themed apparel, further reinforcing its status as a mascot-like figure within the sport.

Safety is another critical aspect of El Toro Loco's operation. While the truck is known for its risky stunts, Monster Jam enforces strict safety protocols to protect drivers and spectators. Trucks are equipped with roll cages, harness systems, and remote ignition interrupters, allowing officials to shut down the engine in emergencies. Tracks are carefully designed with barriers and designated landing zones to minimize danger while still allowing for thrilling performances.

"I AM A PROUD LATINO…IT DOESN'T MATTER WHERE YOU COME FROM, EACH ONE OF US HAS A DREAM AND THAT DREAM FOR ME WAS TO BE A MONSTER JAM DRIVER. IF I COULD DO IT, YOU CAN DO IT."
— DRIVER ARMANDO CASTRO

229
MONSTER JAM
MONSTER JAM

El Toro Loco stands as a symbol of excitement, creativity, and controlled chaos in the world of monster trucks. Its bold design, fearless driving style, and strong fan connection have helped it remain a staple of Monster Jam for over two decades. Whether it's charging across a racecourse or flipping wildly in freestyle, El Toro Loco continues to embody the Latin spirit in this high-octane sport.

70+

THE NUMBER OF DRIVERS THAT HAVE PILOTED EL TORO LOCO.

MONSTER JAM
BKT
BKT
Alkydigger
PIT VIP
FuelTech

EL TORO LOCO IS ONE RAGING BULL WHO CAN SMELL THE FEAR OF ITS COMPETITORS.

MAX-D

Max-D (short for "Maximum Destruction") is one of the most iconic and influential monster trucks in the history of Monster Jam. Created and driven primarily by Tom Meents, the truck debuted in 2003 and quickly became known for its aggressive driving style, cutting-edge design, and record-breaking performances. Over more than two decades of competition, Max-D built a reputation as both a fan favorite and one of the most successful trucks in the sport.

2003

MAX-D FIRST ATTACKED THE TRACKS IN 2003, MARKING THE START OF ONE OF THE MOST DOMINANT RUNS IN MONSTER TRUCK HISTORY.

TOM MEENTS
MAXIMUM
DESTRUCTION

Max-D was originally developed as a successor to Meents' earlier truck, Goldberg, after licensing changes forced a rebrand. The new identity, "Maximum Destruction," reflected Meents' high-risk, high-impact driving approach. The truck was themed as a futuristic, almost robotic machine called "Maximus," emphasizing chaos and power. Its distinctive body style, officially described as a "futuristic SUV," featured sharp angles, an aerodynamic profile, and a striking orange-and-silver paint scheme that made it instantly recognizable in arenas.

A TECHNICAL MARVEL

Technically, Max-D was a highly advanced machine for its time. It typically ran a 540 cubic inch Merlin engine paired with a two-speed transmission and massive 66-inch tires. What set it apart even further was its chassis design. While most monster trucks use mid-engine layouts, some Max-D versions–especially those driven by Meents–featured a front-engine configuration. This unique setup contributed to the truck's balance and helped enable innovative stunts and racing performance.

14 MONSTER JAM WORLD FINALS CHAMPIONSHIPS

DRIVEN BY TOM MEENTS, MAX-D WON AN UNMATCHED 14 MONSTER JAM WORLD FINALS CHAMPIONSHIPS—MORE THAN ANY OTHER DRIVER/TRUCK COMBO.

BKT
BKT
MONSTER JAM

Performance-wise, Max-D was extraordinarily successful. Tom Meents is widely regarded as one of the greatest drivers in monster truck history, and much of his success came behind the wheel of Max-D. He won multiple Monster Jam World Finals Championships, including numerous racing and freestyle titles. Overall, the Max-D team accumulated 15 World Finals Championships across different drivers.

Max-D was also known for pushing the limits of what monster trucks could do. It played a major role in popularizing advanced freestyle tricks, including backflips and complex combinations of jumps and saves. The truck's performances often emphasized controlled chaos–wild-looking runs that were actually carefully executed. This helped redefine freestyle competition and influenced the next generation of drivers.

LASTING LEGACY

Throughout its lifespan, multiple versions of Max-D were built, allowing the team to compete in different tours simultaneously. Other drivers, including Neil Elliott, Blake Granger, and Colton Eichelberger also piloted Max-D trucks, contributing to its legacy and expanding its presence internationally. Despite this, the truck remained closely associated with Meents himself, reinforcing its identity as a driver-focused brand rather than just a vehicle.

In 2013, the truck underwent a major redesign to celebrate its 10th anniversary, introducing more aggressive "spiked" body panels and updated visuals. These changes kept the truck visually fresh while maintaining its core identity. Over time, additional variants such as "Max-D Fire" and anniversary editions further expanded its appeal.

THE MAX-D FAN BASE HAS GROWN SO MUCH THAT MULTIPLE MAX-D MONSTER JAM TRUCKS ARE NOW TOURING. IN 2013, MAX-D RECEIVED A MAKE-OVER TO HELP CELEBRATE A DECADE OF DESTRUCTION WITH TWO BRAND NEW DESIGNS.

RECENT RETIREMENT

After more than 20 years of competition, Max-D was officially retired in 2024, coinciding with Tom Meents' retirement. The decision reflected how closely the truck's identity was tied to its creator and primary driver.

Max-D stands as a heavyweight champion in monster truck history. With its innovative design, dominant competitive record, and role in advancing freestyle performance, it helped shape the modern era of monster truck entertainment. Even after retirement, it remains one of the most recognizable and respected names in the sport.

15

ACROSS RACING AND FREESTYLE (AND MULTIPLE DRIVERS), MAX-D TRUCKS COMBINED FOR 15 TOTAL WORLD FINALS TITLES.

NT
BKT
214

MEGALODON

The Megalodon Monster Truck is one of the most visually striking and mechanically unique competitors in the world of professional monster truck racing. Introduced in 2016 as part of the Monster Jam circuit, Megalodon quickly became a fan favorite thanks to its distinctive shark-inspired design and innovative engineering.

30+ FEET HIGH

IN FREESTYLE EVENTS, MEGALODON CAN LAUNCH MORE THAN THREE STORIES INTO THE AIR DURING ITS BIGGEST TRICKS.

SSES.
great
IT'S GONNA E

FISHY FORM FACTOR

Unlike traditional monster trucks, which typically use a standard rectangular chassis covered by a fiberglass body shell, Megalodon broke the mold with a custom-built tubular frame designed to mimic the skeletal structure of a shark. Its exterior features a flexible, scale-textured body that moves and ripples during motion, giving the illusion that the truck is "swimming" across dirt rather than simply driving over it. This design is not just cosmetic–it contributes to the truck's dynamic movement and helps set it apart in freestyle competitions where creativity and visual appeal are heavily rewarded.

Megalodon's power allows it to perform high jumps, backflips, donuts, and other gravity-defying stunts. Despite its aggressive appearance, the engineering behind Megalodon emphasizes balance and control, crucial for landing tricks safely and maintaining performance consistency.

100+ FEET LONG

WHEN HITTING RAMPS AT SPEED, MEGALODON CAN TRAVEL THE LENGTH OF A BASKETBALL COURT IN A SINGLE LEAP.

MEGALODON'S ENTRANCE SONG IS A METAL COVER OF THE THEME FROM THE MOVIE "JAWS"

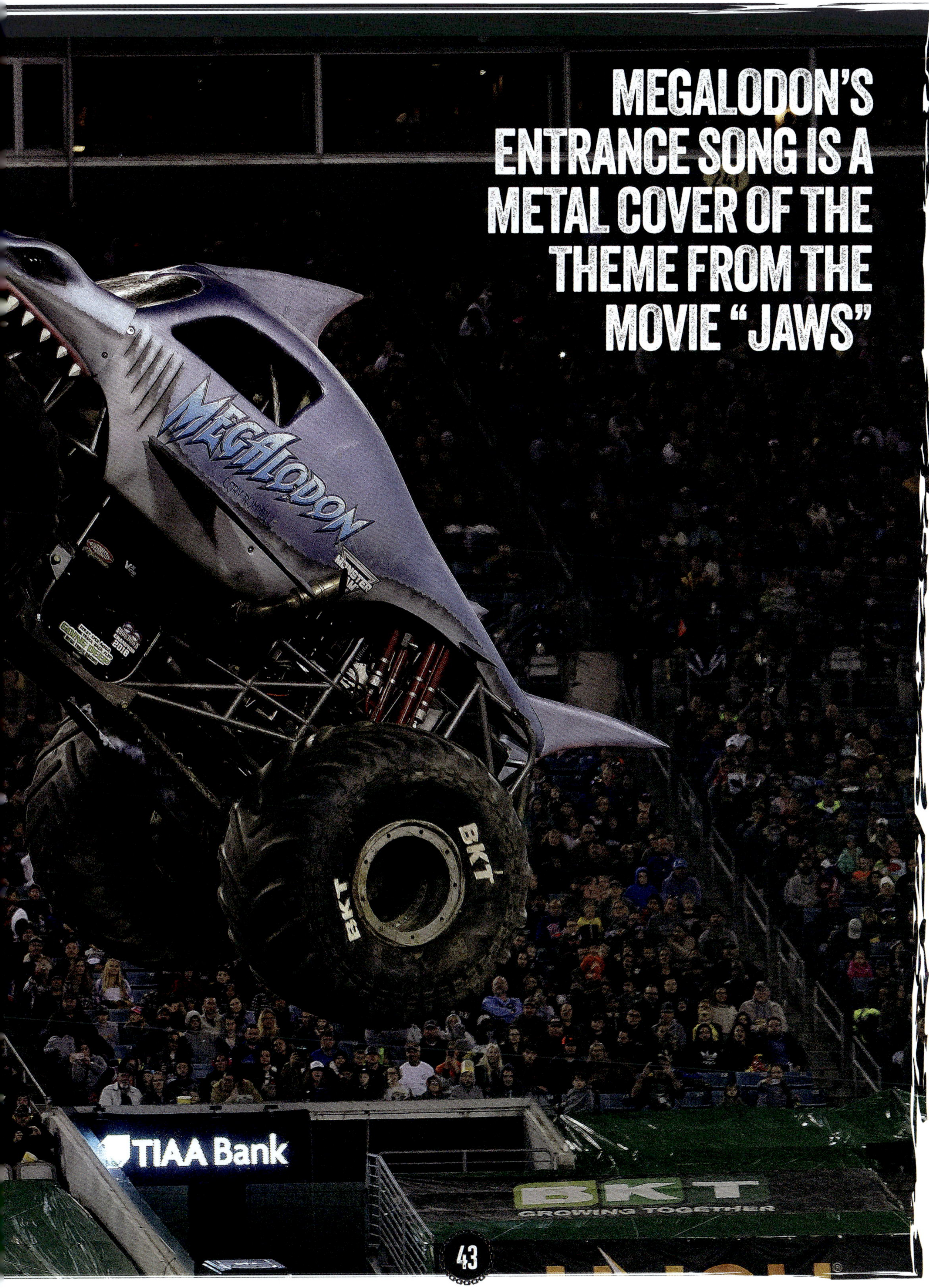

MAKING A SPLASH

One of the defining characteristics of Megalodon is its association with innovation in the sport. In 2019, a variant known as "Megalodon Storm" was introduced as the first amphibious monster truck. This version could transition from land to water, using paddle-like tires to propel itself across the surface. This breakthrough expanded the possibilities for monster truck exhibitions and demonstrated how the sport continues to evolve beyond traditional arena formats.

Drivers play a key role in bringing Megalodon to life. Over the years, several skilled drivers have piloted the truck, each bringing their own style and flair. Their ability to synchronize the truck's unique design with complex tricks is essential to its success in competitions. Freestyle events, in particular, highlight Megalodon's strengths, as judges score based on creativity, execution, and crowd engagement.

AN ACROBATIC AQUATIC

In terms of competition history, Megalodon has achieved multiple event wins and has been a consistent contender in racing and freestyle categories. While it may not always dominate in straight-line racing due to its unconventional structure, it excels in technical and artistic performances. Fans are especially drawn to its fluid movements and the way it visually stands out among more traditional trucks.

For All
GLAZER VISION
FOUNDATION
VIP EXPERIENCE CHECK-IN
VIP EXP
MEGALODON
#MonsterJ

Beyond competition, Megalodon has become a major branding success for Monster Jam. Its shark theme resonates strongly with younger audiences, and it has inspired a wide range of merchandise, including die-cast models, toys, and apparel. The truck's popularity also extends to live events, where its dramatic appearance and performance often make it a centerpiece of the show.

Overall, Megalodon represents a fusion of engineering creativity, entertainment value, and competitive performance. It challenges conventional monster truck design while maintaining the core elements that define the sport—power, spectacle, and excitement. As Monster Jam continues to innovate, Megalodon stands as a symbol of how bold design choices can redefine what fans expect from a monster truck.

2016 DEBUT

DESPITE BEING RELATIVELY NEW COMPARED TO LEGACY TRUCKS, MEGALODON QUICKLY BECAME ONE OF THE MOST RECOGNIZABLE AND INNOVATIVE DESIGNS IN THE SPORT.

BKT

JCB DIGATRON

The JCB DIGatron is among the newest and most distinctive vehicles in the world of monster truck competition, introduced as part of a high-profile partnership between construction equipment manufacturer JCB and the global motorsport entertainment brand Monster Jam. Debuting in January 2024 at the Alamodome in San Antonio, Texas, DIGatron quickly became a standout addition to the Monster Jam fleet due to its unusual design, strong performance, and unique origin story.

TRISTAN ENGLAND
JCB
MONSTER JAM
SIMPSON
BKT
MONSTER JAM

MUSCULAR MECHANICALS

At its core, DIGatron blends the engineering and spectacle of traditional monster trucks with the visual identity of JCB's iconic construction machinery. The truck's body is modeled after a backhoe loader, the piece of equipment that helped define JCB as a company. This inspiration is clearly visible in its styling, which includes a sculpted front loader arm and rear digging bucket elements integrated into the fiberglass shell. Unlike standard monster truck bodies that resemble pickup trucks or fantasy creatures, DIGatron stands out as an industrial-themed vehicle, symbolizing strength, utility, and mechanical power.

Despite its construction-inspired appearance, DIGatron is built on a conventional Monster Jam chassis and meets the same specifications as other elite trucks in the series. Its powerful engine runs on methanol fuel and guzzles it at a rate of about three gallons per minute during competition, reflecting the extreme demands of monster truck performance.

SPECS

10.5 FEET HIGH
12.5 FEET WIDE
17 FEET LONG

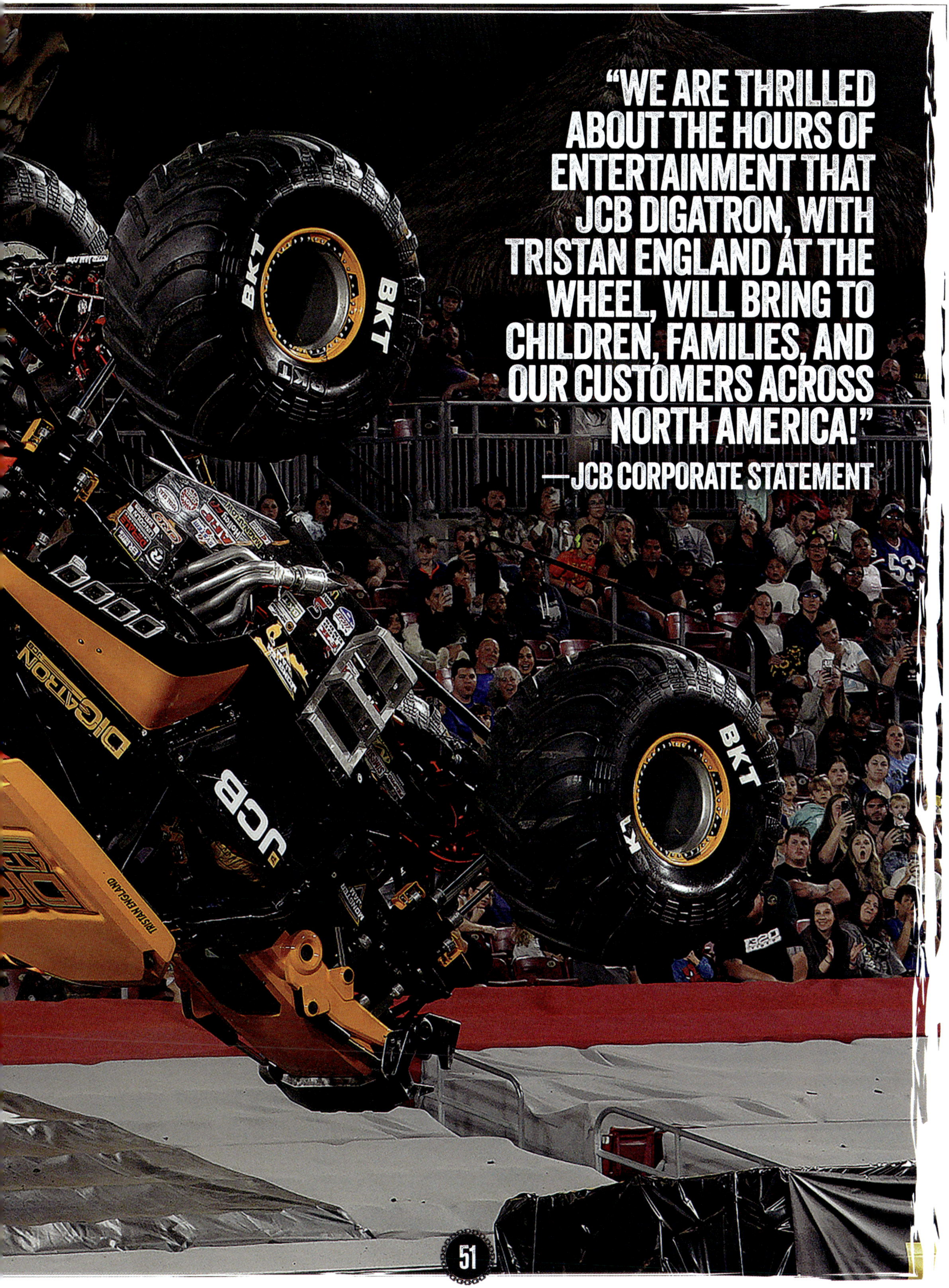

"WE ARE THRILLED ABOUT THE HOURS OF ENTERTAINMENT THAT JCB DIGATRON, WITH TRISTAN ENGLAND AT THE WHEEL, WILL BRING TO CHILDREN, FAMILIES, AND OUR CUSTOMERS ACROSS NORTH AMERICA!"

—JCB CORPORATE STATEMENT

A CONSTRUCTION-THEMED CORNERSTONE

DIGatron's development was a collaborative effort between JCB's engineering team and Monster Jam's organizers, Feld Motor Sports. Interestingly, the idea for the truck originated from a creative concept by Otis Bamford, the grandson of JCB chairman Lord Bamford, who envisioned a construction-themed monster truck. This concept evolved into a full-scale project, highlighting how imaginative ideas can translate into real-world engineering achievements.

In competition, DIGatron has proven to be more than just a novelty design. Driven primarily by Tristan England—a Monster Jam World Finals racing champion—the truck quickly achieved competitive success. In its debut season, it secured multiple event wins and even reached the championship race at Monster Jam World Finals XXIII. By 2025, DIGatron and England captured the Stadium Championship Series West title and won the Skills Challenge World Championship, marking the truck's first world title.

The truck operates with a team of drivers to cover different touring formats. While England competes in major stadium events, other drivers such as Brandon Arthur and Tony Ochs have piloted DIGatron in international and arena competitions. This multi-driver approach allows the truck to appear in events across the globe, increasing its visibility and popularity.

3 GALLONS

JCB DIGATRON BURNS THAT MUCH METHANOL PER MINUTE!

JCB
JCB
JCB
MONSTERJAM.COM

A PRACTICAL SPONSORSHIP

Beyond competition, DIGatron also serves as a marketing and branding tool for JCB. As part of the partnership, JCB equipment is used in building Monster Jam tracks, reinforcing the company's connection to the sport. The truck has also been featured in merchandise, video games, and live demonstrations, helping it reach a broad audience beyond motorsport fans.

The JCB DIGatron monster truck represents an imaginative fusion of industrial design and high-performance motorsport. Its backhoe-inspired appearance, powerful engineering, and early competitive success have made it a memorable addition to Monster Jam. More than just a racing vehicle, DIGatron symbolizes innovation, collaboration, and the creative possibilities that emerge when different industries intersect.

SPIN MASTER

SON-UVA DIGGER

Son-uva Digger represents the next generation of one of the most iconic names in the sport. Built as a successor to the legendary Grave Digger lineage, Son-uva Digger carries forward a legacy of innovation, showmanship, and competitive excellence while carving out its own identity in the modern era of monster truck events.

The truck was introduced in 2011 and is driven by Ryan Anderson, the son of Dennis Anderson, who created the original Grave Digger. This father-son connection is central to the truck's identity–hence the name "Son-uva Digger." It symbolizes both a continuation of tradition and a passing of the torch, blending old-school monster truck culture with contemporary performance and style.

MAGNAFLOW
NGK
K&N
VP
FELPRO
WISECO
CROWER
LINCOLN WELDERS
HAWK

AN AMERICAN ICON

Visually, Son-uva Digger stands out immediately. Its body design is inspired by the classic 1950 Chevrolet panel van, but with a heavily customized, aggressive look. The paint scheme features a striking mix of black, blue, and purple flames over a distressed, rusted aesthetic that pays homage to the original Grave Digger's rough, scrapyard roots. The truck also includes detailed graphics such as faux patina, giving it a weathered, rebellious personality that resonates with fans.

Underneath its eye-catching exterior lies a highly advanced piece of machinery. Like most top-tier monster trucks, Son-uva Digger rides on a custom-built tubular steel chassis designed for strength and flexibility. The suspension system, featuring massive nitrogen-charged shocks, enables it to absorb the impact of spectacular stunts and jumps.

A FEROCIOUS FREESTYLER

Son-uva Digger competes in Monster Jam events, where it participates in several competition categories including racing, freestyle, and skills challenges. In racing, trucks compete head-to-head on short, technical tracks that require both speed and precision. But it's in freestyle, where drivers are judged on the creativity, difficulty, and execution of their moves, that Son-uva Digger sets itself apart.

MONSTER JAM

Ryan Anderson has become known for his aggressive and innovative driving style, often pushing the limits of what monster trucks can do. Son-uva Digger is particularly famous for performing advanced tricks such as backflips, bicycle moves (balancing on two wheels), and sky wheelies. These maneuvers require not only raw power but also precise control and timing. Anderson's willingness to take risks has earned him multiple championships and a reputation as one of the top drivers in the sport.

GROUNDBREAKING GUTS

Another defining feature of Son-uva Digger is its role in evolving the expectations of monster truck performances. Earlier generations of trucks focused primarily on crushing cars and straight-line racing. In contrast, Son-uva Digger represents the modern era, where freestyle performance and technical tricks are central to the spectacle. Its design and capabilities reflect this shift, emphasizing maneuverability and stunt potential as much as brute force.

"15 YEARS OF SON-UVA DIGGER. AND AFTER ALL THOSE YEARS I THINK IT'S TIME FOR ME TO SLOW IT DOWN..... SIKE! IT'S TIME TO KICK IT IN HIGH GEAR!"

— DRIVER RYAN ANDERSON OFFICIAL FACEBOOK PAGE

MONSTER JAM
LAS VEGAS
MONSTER JAM
MONSTERJAM.COM
Budweiser

Fan engagement is also a big part of the truck's success. Son-uva Digger is a staple at live events, where it often appears in pit parties that allow fans to see the truck up close, meet the driver, and learn more about how it works. Its unique design and family legacy make it especially appealing to both longtime fans and newcomers.

Son-uva Digger is monster truck royalty of sorts, and more than just a monster truck, it is a symbol of continuity and evolution within the sport. By combining heritage with cutting-edge performance, it honors its roots while pushing the boundaries of what monster trucks can achieve in 2026 and beyond.

SPECS

ENGINE DISPLACEMENT: 565 CUBIC INCHES (BIG-BLOCK SUPERCHARGED V8)

WEIGHT: 10,000 LBS (4,535 KG) PRETTY HEAVY FOR A "SON"

TOP SPEED: 70 MPH (113 KM/H)

HEIGHT: SON-UVA DIGGER STANDS OVER 12 FEET (3.6 M) TALL!

MORGAN & MORGAN
AMERICA'S LARGEST INJURY LAW FIRM

ZOMBIE

Zombie is one of the more distinctive themed vehicles in the world of professional monster truck racing and freestyle exhibitions. Built for spectacle as much as competition, it combines aggressive styling, theatrical presentation, and high-powered engineering to deliver performances designed to thrill live audiences, particularly in events like Monster Jam.

2013

ZOMBIE MADE ITS MONSTER JAM DEBUT IN 2013 AS PART OF FELD ENTERTAINMENT'S EXPANSION OF THEMED CHARACTER TRUCKS, QUICKLY BECOMING A FEARFUL FAN FAVORITE IN THE TOURING LINEUP.

20
26
THE TRUCKS
MONSTER TRUCKS
MADNESS AND BADNESS

A LOOK THAT'LL GRAB YOU

At its core, Zombie follows the standard engineering blueprint of modern monster trucks, but what sets it apart is its theme and visual identity. The body is sculpted to resemble a decayed, undead creature emerging from a horror-inspired world. The design typically includes torn "flesh" textures, exposed bone imagery, glowing eyes, exaggerated facial expressions that evoke a cartoonish but unsettling zombie aesthetic, and even outreaching arms! This theatrical approach is intentional, as monster trucks use strong character branding to build fan recognition and emotional engagement, especially among younger audiences.

Zombie is part of a broader tradition in monster truck culture where vehicles are designed as characters rather than just machines. Alongside trucks like Grave Digger, El Toro Loco, and Max-D, Zombie helps create a narrative-driven environment where each truck feels like a competitor with personality. In live shows, announcers often amplify this identity by giving the truck voice-like traits or storylines, framing it as an "undead machine" that refuses to be destroyed no matter how many crashes it endures.

ZOMBIE
TRAVIS MOWERY

In competition settings, Zombie participates in standard Monster Jam formats, which include racing, two-wheel skills challenges, and freestyle rounds. Freestyle is where Zombie and similar trucks shine most, as drivers attempt to maximize airtime, execute stunts, and maintain momentum while the crowd reacts in real time. Judges and fans score performances based on difficulty, execution, variety, and crowd engagement.

A RELENTLESS COMPETITOR

One of the defining features of the Zombie's appeal is its durability in appearance and performance storytelling. While monster trucks are heavily engineered for safety and repairability, they are also expected to endure dramatic destruction. The Zombie theme reinforces this expectation–crashes, rollovers, and smashed body panels are not failures but part of the narrative of an "undead" machine that keeps returning to action. This creates a feedback loop where damage enhances the character rather than diminishing it.

"LEAVE 'EM IN THE DUST, VICTORY OR BUST."

— DRIVER BARI MUSAWWIR ON INSTAGRAM

ZOMBIE
BKT
BKT
THE BLACK

Drivers of Zombie truck are highly trained professionals who must master not only vehicle control but also showmanship. They must balance competitive strategy with entertainment value, deciding when to take risks for higher scores or crowd reaction. Precision throttle control, brake timing, and spatial awareness are critical, especially during freestyle segments where one mistake can lead to a rollover or mechanical failure.

ZOMBIES DON'T DIE

Over time, Zombie has become a recognizable figure in the Monster Jam circuit, contributing to the growing popularity of themed monster trucks in motorsport entertainment. It represents the blending of engineering, performance art, and theatrical storytelling that defines modern monster truck shows. Fans often associate it with high-energy performances and dramatic recoveries, reinforcing its identity as a relentless, horror-inspired competitor.

Zombie is more than a decorated vehicle—it is the epitome of a carefully crafted entertainment persona built on top of advanced automotive engineering. Within the world of Monster Jam, it stands as a vivid example of how mechanical sport can merge with character-driven spectacle to create a unique and enduring form of live entertainment.

BARI MUSAWWIR

IS ONE OF ITS MOST RECOGNIZED DRIVERS WHO WAS BRAVE ENOUGH TO DRIVE THE UNDEAD MONSTROSITY. THE TRUCK'S "ZOMBIE" THEME IS EMPHASIZED IN FREESTYLE EVENTS, WHERE CRASHES AND RECOVERIES ARE FRAMED AS PART OF ITS RELENTLESS RESILIENCE.

ZOMBIE
MONSTER JAM

MONSTER MUTT PACK

The Monster Mutt family is one of the most recognizable "pack" of trucks in the history of Monster Jam. Known for their oversized dog-themed bodies, floppy ears, wagging tails, and playful personalities, the Monster Mutt trucks became fan favorites because they combined the power of traditional monster trucks with a fun design that appealed to children and dog lovers of all ages. Since their debut in 2003, the Monster Mutt pack has competed in racing, freestyle, skills competitions, and championship events around the world.

DID YOU KNOW?

THE MONSTER MUTT PACK EXPANDED INTO SEVERAL DOG BREEDS OF TRUCKS, MANY OF WHICH HAVE BECOME AMONG THE MOST POPULAR MERCH IN THE MONSTER JAM UNIVERSE.

BKT

The origin of Monster Mutt traces back to the early 2000s, when promoters wanted to create a new truck character. Before the truck officially appeared, there had been plans for a separate truck called "The Incredible Hulk" that would use a 1950 Mercury-style body. Another canceled idea called "Junkyard Dog" also existed during development. Eventually, designers combined the Mercury body with a dog theme, adding large ears, a tongue, teeth, and a red dog collar to create the first Monster Mutt. The truck made its competition debut in Oakland, California, in January 2003.

The original Monster Mutt was painted brown and styled after a Labrador retriever. Unlike many monster trucks that used intimidating or aggressive appearances, Monster Mutt was designed to look playful and friendly. The entrance music, "Who Let the Dogs Out" by the Baha Men, quickly became leashed to the truck and helped create a lively atmosphere during events. Fans especially enjoyed seeing the truck's tail bounce as it drove over obstacles and crushed cars during freestyle runs.

"WHO, WHO, WHO, WHO, WHO?":

PERHAPS THE MOST SUNG ALONG ENTRANCE MUSIC IN ALL OF MONSTER JAM, THE MONSTER MUTT TRUCKS CHARGE INTO ARENAS TO THE HIT SONG BY BAHA MEN, "WHO LET THE DOGS OUT."

MONSTER MUTT
BKT
BKT
MONSTER JAM
MONSTER JAM

Mechanically, Monster Mutt was built like a top-tier competitive monster truck. Like other Monster Jam trucks, it could perform wheelies, donuts, high jumps, and backflips in freestyle competitions. Over the years, the truck evolved from its original 1950 Mercury-inspired body into a fully 3D dog design, introduced in 2016. This redesign featured more realistic teeth, facial features, and sculpted body panels to make the truck appear even more like a giant dog.

One reason the Monster Mutt pack became so successful was the creation of several spin-off trucks. The first major addition was Monster Mutt Dalmatian, introduced in 2007. The Dalmatian version used the same dog concept but featured white paint with black spots to resemble a Dalmatian dog. It quickly became popular with younger fans and often appeared in promotional material. Drivers such as Candice Jolly and Cynthia Gauthier helped make the Dalmatian one of the most visible female-driven trucks in Monster Jam history.

Another member of the family, Monster Mutt Rottweiler, debuted in 2011. This version had a darker, more aggressive appearance inspired by the Rottweiler dog breed. The truck featured sharper teeth, black-and-brown coloring, and a fiercer personality compared to the original brown Monster Mutt. Drivers including Charles Benns and Rod Schmidt piloted the truck in racing and freestyle events, where it became known for hard hits and exciting saves during competitions.

In 2016, Monster Jam introduced Monster Mutt Junkyard Dog, a temporary spin-off designed to resemble an old rusty junkyard vehicle. Unlike the newer cartoon-style mutts, Junkyard Dog retained the classic Mercury body shape and gave longtime fans a nostalgic reminder of the original Monster Mutt design. Although the truck only competed for a short time, it developed a cult following among enthusiasts who preferred the older body style.

GIANT
SUBS
BKT
BKT
OPTIMA
Lincoln
Coan

The Monster Mutt family performed strongly in major Monster Jam competitions. Perhaps the greatest achievements came in 2010 when veteran driver Charlie Pauken won the Monster Jam World Finals Freestyle Championship in Las Vegas driving the original Monster Mutt. His run included massive jumps, smooth momentum, and crowd-pleasing stunts that earned some of the highest scores of the night. This victory proved that Monster Mutt was more than just a novelty truck and could compete with legendary names like Grave Digger and Maximum Destruction.

Over the years, Monster Mutt trucks regularly appeared at Monster Jam World Finals events and toured internationally. Drivers rotated frequently, allowing many competitors to gain experience behind the wheel. The truck family also became one of the best-selling merchandise brands in Monster Jam, appearing on toys, video games, clothing, and die-cast collectibles. Its popularity with children helped introduce new generations of fans to monster truck racing.

Today, the Monster Mutt family remains an important part of monster truck culture. While some versions have been retired or temporarily shelved, the trucks continue to have a strong fanbase. Their combination of creative design, competitive performance, and memorable personalities has made them one of the defining attractions in modern Monster Jam history. From freestyle championships to packed stadium performances, Monster Mutt and its canine-themed cohorts helped transform monster trucks from simple racing machines into larger-than-life entertainment icons.

MONSTER JAM
BKT

LUCAS STABILIZER

Sponsored by Lucas Oil Products, this beast was designed to promote the company's automotive lubricants while competing in major monster truck competitions across the country. The first version of the truck debuted in 2011 and was dubbed the Lucas Oil Crusader. By then the Lucas Oil brand had already built a strong reputation in racing, off-road performance, and motorsports broadcasting, making monster trucks a slick extension of its marketing presence.

2022

DEBUT MONSTER JAM SEASON.

2026
THE TRUCKS
MONSTER TRUCKS
MADNESS AND BADNESS
HI-PERFORMANCE LUCAS PRODUCTS INC.
LUCAS STABILIZER
LUCAS OIL PRODUCTS
INDIANAPOLIS, IN
USDOT 07171989
MONSTER JAM
BKT
BKT
MAGNAFLOW
Holley

Designed as a custom Peterbilt semi-truck, the Lucas Oil Stabilizer pays homage to the company's trucking roots, and has been driven primarily by Cynthia Gauthier since 2022. One of the major attractions of the truck is its versatility: it participated in racing brackets where trucks competed head-to-head on short dirt tracks filled with ramps and crushed cars.

In freestyle competition, the truck's performance became even more exciting. Freestyle events rewarded creativity, wheelies, donuts, sky wheelies, and large jumps that wowed fans and impressed judges. The Lucas Oil truck gained acclaim for aggressive driving styles and crowd-pleasing stunts.

Fans love the truck not only for its powerful performance but also for its distinctive semi-truck cab look and red-and-white branding that prominently displayed the Lucas Oil logo. Its visibility at televised events helped strengthen the relationship between corporate sponsorship and monster truck culture.

Despite mechanical wear and tear, and the demanding nature of competition, the Lucas Oil Stabilizer truck has maintained a reputation for reliability and entertainment value. Today, it remains a slick example of how sponsorship, engineering, and showmanship combine to shape modern monster truck events and excite fans everywhere.

BODY STYLE

SEMI-TRUCK INSPIRED PETERBILT CONCEPT INCLUDING CHROME STACKS, FUEL TANKS, AND A HEAVY-DUTY GRILLE (FIRST OF ITS KIND IN MONSTER JAM).

MONSTER JAM
2002
BKT
BKT
LINSEY READ
LUCAS OIL PRODUCTS
INDIANAPOLIS, IN
USDOT 07171989
LUCAS STABILIZER
LUCAS OIL
MONSTER JAM

MOHAWK WARRIOR

Mohawk Warrior debuted in 2010 and quickly became a standout due to its unique appearance: a black-and-purple Cadillac Escalade body topped with a large fiberglass mohawk, inspired by its original driver George Balhan's signature hairstyle and persona.

HIGH-SPEED MILESTONE: **MOHAWK WARRIOR BECAME PART OF MONSTER JAM'S PUSH INTO SPEED-FOCUSED COMPETITION, WITH BRYCE KENNY PILOTING IT IN EVENTS WHERE MONSTER TRUCKS BROKE THE 100 MPH BARRIER IN EXHIBITION DRAG RACING-STYLE RUNS, A MAJOR BENCHMARK FOR THE SPORT'S EVOLUTION.**

MONSTERJAM.COM

From the beginning, Mohawk Warrior was designed to feel like more than just a machine—it was a character-driven truck with a rebellious, warrior-like identity. Its early years featured Balhan as the primary driver, and the truck became closely associated with his driving style: aggressive racing lines, high-risk freestyle attempts, and crowd-pleasing energy. The truck first appeared at the Monster Jam World Finals in 2010 and became a regular competitor in subsequent seasons.

Over time, Mohawk Warrior evolved both mechanically and visually. It moved through several chassis upgrades and tire generations while maintaining its signature mohawk roof structure. The truck's body style remained based on a Cadillac Escalade, but its paint scheme and sponsorships changed, most notably becoming Great Clips Mohawk Warrior during its later years. This partnership became part of its identity, especially in the 2016-2024 era.

After Balhan's retirement in 2016, Bryce Kenny took over driving duties. Under Kenny, Mohawk Warrior reached new competitive heights, regularly competing in Monster Jam Stadium Series events and World Finals appearances. The truck earned multiple freestyle and racing wins and became known for spectacular stunts, including backflips, massive jumps, and record-setting speed runs. One of its most notable achievements was helping set a monster truck speed record by exceeding 100 mph during a special event in 2020!

The truck also gained attention for its dramatic and sometimes unpredictable freestyle moments. Its tall mohawk structure made it visually distinctive but also slightly top-heavy, contributing to memorable saves, rolls, and crashes that became highlight-reel staples.

By 2024, Mohawk Warrior had completed its competitive run and was officially retired from active Monster Jam competition. Despite this, it remains one of the most iconic trucks in the sport's modern era.

SIGNATURE SPONSORSHIP IDENTITY: DURING ITS LATER COMPETITIVE YEARS, THE TRUCK COMPETED AS "GREAT CLIPS MOHAWK WARRIOR," MAKING IT ONE OF THE MORE RECOGNIZABLE SPONSORED TRUCKS IN MONSTER JAM STADIUM TOURS DUE TO ITS CONSISTENT BRANDING AND HIGH VISIBILITY.

FREESTYLE REPUTATION AND DURABILITY: THE TRUCK EARNED A REPUTATION FOR DRAMATIC FREESTYLE PERFORMANCES, OFTEN INVOLVING HARD LANDINGS, NEAR-ROLLOVERS, AND HEAVY CHASSIS ABUSE; YET STILL FREQUENTLY RETURNED TO COMPETITION, WHICH BECAME A DEFINING PART OF ITS "WARRIOR" IDENTITY.

SOLDIER FORTUNE

Soldier Fortune proudly debuted in 2015 as a tribute to members of the United States Armed Forces. Built and operated by veteran driver Chad Fortune, who also played a key role in developing its concept as a way to honor service members through motorsport entertainment, it quickly became recognizable for its military-inspired design and patriotic theme.

2015

DEBUT YEAR OF SOLIDER FORTUNE.

P14
SOLDIER FORTUNE

The original Soldier Fortune features a camouflaged paint scheme and a body style that resembles a heavily armored military vehicle, often compared to a futuristic combat truck. Its design emphasizes ruggedness, with a tank-like aesthetic, oversized tires, and aggressive detailing that fits the Monster Jam style of larger-than-life machines. The truck is built on a specialized tube chassis designed for durability under extreme conditions, including jumps, flips, and car-crushing impacts typical of Monster Jam competitions.

In 2016, Monster Jam introduced a related truck called Soldier Fortune Black Ops, which expanded the concept. This version features a mostly black colorway and is meant to represent elite special operations military units. It was initially driven by U.S. Army veteran Tony Ochs, further reinforcing the military tribute theme.

Soldier Fortune has remained part of the Monster Jam lineup in various forms, including special variations like "Ice" and other seasonal designs. The Soldier Fortune fleet stands out in Monster Jam for combining entertainment with a respectful homage to military service, blending patriotism with the high-energy spectacle of monster truck performances.

GOD BLESS AMERICA

SOLIDER FORTUNE IS THE BEST-KNOWN TRUCK THAT CELEBRATES AMERICAN MILITARY PERSONNEL.

SOLDIER FORTUNE BLACK OPS
BKT
K&N

SPARKLE SMASH

In a reverse of the typical process, Sparkle Smash actually began life as a popular Spin Master toy concept before being turned into a real competitive truck due to strong fan demand and brisk merch sales.

2024

DEBUT YEAR OF SPARKLE SMASH.

Kayla Blood
MONSTER JAM
MONSTERJAM.COM
BKT

Best known for its bright unicorn-themed design and its focus on high-energy, crowd-friendly performances, Sparkle Smash officially debuted in 2024 under Feld Motorsports and quickly became one of the more recognizable newer entries in the Monster Jam lineup.

Visually, Sparkle Smash stands out immediately. It features a custom unicorn body style with a vibrant mix of pink, purple, and blue accents, often with glitter-like graphics that reinforce its "sparkle" theme. One of its signature details is the unicorn horn mounted on the cab, which in some versions is capable of special effects like spreading confetti or doing fabulous celebratory stunts during shows. The overall design is meant to be playful and fantasy-inspired, making it especially popular with younger female fans while still being built for serious monster truck competition.

A notable aspect of Sparkle Smash is its rotating driver lineup. The truck is often operated by multiple drivers across different tours and regions, including stadium and arena series events. This approach allows it to appear frequently at shows around the world while also showcasing different driving styles. The team behind it has also emphasized "girl power" representation, contributing to its popularity among diverse audiences.

In Monster Jam culture, Sparkle Smash has become more than just a truck—it's a character-driven brand. It represents a mix of power and flashy personality, combining aggressive driving with a lighthearted, colorful identity. Fans often recognize it not just for its performance, but for its branding, merchandise, and strong visual identity. Since its debut, it has become a staple in modern Monster Jam events and continues to grow in popularity as part of the current generation of trucks.

Kayla Blood
Sparkle SMASH
MONSTER JAM
SALT

WHIPLASH

Whiplash debuted in 2018 as part of an effort to expand the sport's diversity and storytelling through themed vehicles. The truck is built on a custom CRD Generation 3 chassis and originally featured a 1941 Willys pickup body style, giving it a classic, vintage-inspired look while still housing modern high-performance components like a 540 cubic-inch Merlin engine and a two-speed Coan transmission.

From the jump, Whiplash was closely associated with driver Brianna Mahon, who became its primary and most recognizable competitor. The truck was designed not only for competition but also to represent empowerment within Monster Jam, as it was one of the few trucks in the series consistently driven by women throughout its career. This made Whiplash stand out in a field where many trucks are driven by multiple rotating drivers and more masculine branding.

"IT'S MY OWN PERSONAL BRAND...IT'S GOT COWBOY BOOTS ON IT AND A LEATHER TOOLING LOOK. I'M BIG INTO RODEO AND WESTERN FASHION."

— DRIVER BRIANNA MAHON

On the competitive front, Whiplash battled in Monster Jam stadium and arena series events from 2018 through 2022, taking part in racing, skills challenges, and freestyle competitions. One of its most notable early achievements came when it earned a freestyle win in San Diego during its debut season, and it quickly became known for its aggressive driving style and occasional high-risk stunts. In 2019, the truck gained attention at the Monster Jam World Finals XX, where it placed third in freestyle.

Over its lifespan, Whiplash appeared in multiple Monster Jam World Finals events and notched decent if unspectacular results. The truck's design and branding emphasized a bold, non-stereotypical aesthetic and is a concious effort to shift away from typical bright "pink" gender-coded designs and instead used a more rugged and distinctive visual identity.

Whiplash was operated by other drivers when Mahon was unavailable, including Cynthia Gauthier and Kayla Blood, especially during injury recovery periods and touring schedules. The truck even made international appearances, including events in Australia.

By 2022, Whiplash was phased out of regular competition following Mahon's maternity leave and shifting Monster Jam lineup decisions. While it has not returned as an active competitive truck, it remains part of Monster Jam history and continues to be recognized among fans, including appearances in Monster Jam video games and merch.

2022

BRIANNA MAHON CAPTURED THE MONSTER JAM STADIUM CHAMPIONSHIP SERIES EAST TITLE THIS YEAR DRIVING WHIPLASH.

JESTER

Jester is known for its bright, chaotic "clown/jester" theme and highly variable paint schemes. It is owned by Tomfoolery Motorsports and has been a consistent presence in professional monster truck events since its debut in the mid-2010s.

Jester made its official debut in 2015, with Matt Pagliarulo as its primary driver and lead builder/owner involvement from his family team. The truck is based on a 2013 Cadillac Escalade body style, which gives it a large, luxury-SUV shape that contrasts humorously with its circus-themed design. Because of this, fans sometimes nickname it the "Jestalade."

REBEL WITH A CAUSE

JESTER IS AMONG THE MOST BELOVED INDEPENDENT MONSTER TRUCKS OUTSIDE OF MONSTER JAM.

S Assure
CLUB 238
JESTER
BKT
S Assure
UB 138

The concept behind Jester was developed years before its debut. According to its creators, the idea came from discussions about building a truck with a playful, clown-inspired identity. The jester character–traditionally associated with colorful costumes, comedy, and unpredictability–was chosen as a perfect fit for a monster truck designed to entertain both in racing and freestyle events. The signature design element is the oversized jester hat mounted on the truck body, which visually reinforces the theme and helps it stand out on the track.

Mechanically, Jester is built for high-performance competition. It uses a custom tube chassis (later upgraded over time), a large-displacement Chevrolet racing engine, and heavy-duty drivetrain components typical of professional monster trucks.

One of Jester's defining features is its constantly changing liveries. Unlike many trucks with a single fixed design, Jester frequently appears in different color schemes: green, purple, blue, red, silver, and themed designs for holidays or special events. These variations are often revealed at major competitions like the Monster Jam World Finals or special stadium series events. This evolving look has become part of its identity, making it one of the more visually unpredictable trucks in the sport.

Over the years, Jester has competed in multiple Monster Jam stadium series and arena events, as well as special showcase appearances. It has also been driven by guest drivers within the Pagliarulo family team, including younger family members gaining experience in select events. The truck has earned a reputation as a strong mid-pack to competitive freestyle performer, with occasional event wins and standout runs.

Today, Jester remains an active and recognizable entry in monster truck competition, valued less for championship dominance and more for its personality-driven design, family-run team story, and ever-changing visual style that keeps fans guessing what version will show up next.

JESTER

KRAKEN

Kraken is known for its distinctive ocean-themed design and its presence in major U.S. monster truck circuits like Monster Jam and independent touring series. Also built and operated by Tomfoolery Motorsports, Kraken debuted in 2018 and quickly became recognizable for blending aggressive performance with a striking visual identity inspired by the mythical sea creature it is named after.

Kraken's name comes from the legendary Scandinavian sea monster described in maritime folklore as a massive, tentacled creature capable of dragging ships underwater. That mythological influence is central to the truck's branding: its bodywork features a squid-like aesthetic, often with glowing eyes, tentacle graphics, and a "deep-sea predator" color scheme that has included green, blue, and purple variations over time.

MONSTER JAM
MONSTER JAM
UTAH SPORTS COMMISSION
MONSTER JAM
SHOWDOWN

The truck is primarily driven by Nick Pagliarulo, with occasional appearances by other drivers in the team, and it competes across stadium series and arena events. Over the years, Kraken has developed a reputation for aggressive freestyle performances, including high-risk aerial maneuvers and crashes that have become part of its competitive identity. It has also earned freestyle event wins in multiple cities, helping establish it as more than just a visually interesting entry.

One of Kraken's notable features in the monster truck world is its evolving body design. Unlike many trucks that remain visually consistent for years, Kraken has undergone several redesigns, including a shift from its original green squid concept to alternate color schemes used in special events and World Finals appearances. These changes keep the truck visually fresh and help maintain its branding as a "living" sea monster that evolves season to season.

Overall, Kraken stands out in the monster truck scene for combining strong competitive performance with a highly thematic identity, making it both a fan favorite and a recognizable fixture in modern monster truck events.

2020

THE YEAR THIS TRUCK WAS INTRODUCED AS PART OF MONSTER JAM'S FANTASY-CREATURE LINEUP.

PIT VIPER
STARR
CREATIONS
ORTHERN
+ EQUIPMENT
ntool.com

AVENGER

Avenger is one of the most recognizable and respected vehicles in the world of monster truck racing and freestyle competition. Driven by veteran Jim Koehler, Avenger became famous for its aggressive driving style, huge air, and unforgettable colorway. Fans across the country know the truck for its exciting performances at major monster truck events and stadium shows.

Avenger first appeared in the late 1990s and quickly earned a reputation as a serious competitor. Koehler became known as "Mr. Excitement" because of his unpredictable, all-out freestyle driving style. Unlike many factory-backed teams, he built Avenger as an independent operation and still managed to compete with the biggest names in the sport for decades. His truck became famous for its bright green paint, flaming skull graphics, and wild save attempts during freestyle runs.

20
26
THE TRUCKS
MONSTER TRUCKS
MADNESS AND BADNESS
AVENGER
LUCAS OIL PRODUCTS INC.
Coan
HOOKER HARNESS
NGK
MSD
MONSTER JAM
BKT
OFFICIAL TIRE OF MONSTER JAM

One of the biggest moments of his career came at the 2003 Monster Jam World Finals, when he won the Freestyle Championship with a score of 37, becoming the first freestyle champion not named Dennis Anderson or Tom Meents. He won a second World Finals freestyle title in 2011 after a dramatic tie-breaker victory.

Koehler is also notable for his incredible longevity. He competed in every Monster Jam World Finals event from the beginning of the series in 2000 through the mid-2020s, something very few drivers have accomplished. In 2025, he was inducted into the International Monster Truck Hall of Fame in recognition of his influence on the sport.

Today, Avenger remains an important part of monster truck history. Its unique design, exciting driving style, and loyal fan base have helped it stay popular for decades. Many monster truck fans consider Avenger one of the greatest independent trucks ever built, and its legacy continues to inspire future drivers and teams throughout the sport.

1997

AVENGER DEBUTED IN 1997, AND HAS BEEN DRIVEN BY THE FIERCE AND BELOVED JIM KOEHLER EVER SINCE.

AVENGER
Coan
Racing
R.J.S.
RACING EQUIPMENT, INC.
CANIDAE

EXCALIBER

Excaliber is a long-running and well-known independent entry in the American monster truck scene, with a history that stretches back to the mid-1980s. It debuted in 1985, originally built by Dave Marquart and Mike Nickel, and quickly became notable for being one of the earlier professionally engineered monster trucks rather than a simple "modified pickup" build. Excaliber changed ownership and design multiple times, but it maintained its identity as a competitive, fan-favorite machine across several eras of monster truck competition.

The truck's name is inspired by the legendary sword of King Arthur, though it is intentionally spelled "Excaliber," giving it a slightly unique branding twist. In its earliest form, Excaliber was based on a Chevrolet pickup (initially a 1978-era K20 platform) and used conventional monster truck construction for its time: a heavily modified chassis, oversized tires, and a powerful big-block Chevrolet engine. Like many trucks of its era, it was built to compete in both racing and freestyle exhibitions, which were rapidly becoming the two main attractions in monster truck events during the 1980s and 1990s.

BKT
BKT
UTAH SPOR
COMMISSION

One of Excaliber's notable technical distinctions is that it evolved alongside major changes in monster truck engineering. Early versions were closer to stock-based builds, but later iterations transitioned into fully custom tube-frame chassis designs, improved suspension systems, and more powerful engines until it eventually reached modern configurations using high-performance Chevrolet-based powerplants and racing transmissions like the Turbo 400 or Powerglide setups. These upgrades allowed the truck to remain competitive as monster trucks became faster, higher-flying, and more extreme in freestyle performance.

Over the years, Excaliber passed through several owners and drivers, including noted driver Charlie Pauken, a well-known name in the monster truck world. Its competitive history includes appearances in various independent events and tournament-style competitions, sometimes facing iconic trucks like BIGFOOT and other major series entries. While it was never always a headline "touring superstar" like some Monster Jam factory teams, Excaliber built a reputation as a respected, consistent competitor with strong regional and independent event presence.

In recent years, the name has been revived under new ownership (Tomfoolery Motorsports), continuing the tradition with updated hardware and modern components. Overall, Excaliber stands out as a "bridge" truck in monster truck history–connecting the early experimental era of modified pickups to the highly engineered, purpose-built machines seen in modern competition.

EXCALIBUR
BKT

BAILEY CIRCUIT

Bailey Circuit entered the big top in 2025 and has quickly become a star attraction. Owned by Feld Motorsports and sponsored by Ringling Bros. and Barnum & Bailey Circus, its design is inspired by Bailey, the robotic dog mascot featured in the reimagined Ringling circus shows.

ROBOT DOGS FTW!

WHEN RINGLING BROS. AND BARNUM & BAILEY RETURNED TO TOURING, THEY MADE A CONSCIOUS AND COMPASSIONATE CHOICE TO OPERATE WITHOUT ANIMALS. TO KEEP THE BELOVED TRADITION OF CIRCUS ANIMALS ALIVE FOR A NEW GENERATION, THE COMPANY INTRODUCED BAILEY, A RASCALLY ROBOTIC MASCOT.

Photo by Charley Gallay/Getty Images

Built on a custom 2008 Ford F-150 body and using a CRD chassis with a powerful 540ci Merlin engine, the truck officially premiered in Raleigh, North Carolina, on July 26, 2025. Veteran Monster Jam driver Brianna Mahon was selected as the main driver for the debut. Mahon was already popular among fans because of her earlier success driving Scooby-Doo, Whiplash, and other Monster Jam trucks.

Because of its playful appearance and vibrant colorway, Bailey Circuit stands out like, well, a ringmaster. The truck features bright pink and yellow colors, dog ears on the roof, a tongue sticking out from the grille, and even moving cartoon eyes (like in the movie "Cars") used during pit parties. A slinky-style tail is attached to the rear. These features were designed to resemble Bailey the robot dog and make the truck visually appealing to younger audiences and families.

Many fans believe Bailey Circuit effectively replaced the Scooby-Doo truck in Monster Jam, especially since Mahon previously drove Scooby-Doo and the truck disappeared from the 2026 schedule after Bailey Circuit debuted. Some longtime fans have criticized the design as overly commercial or too child-focused, while others appreciate its colorful style and connection to the circus brand.

Discussions online show mixed reactions: some people call it creative and fun, while others see it as a sign of Monster Jam shifting toward younger audiences. In any case, many comments agree that children love the truck and that it succeeds as an entertainment-focused character vehicle.

By 2026, Bailey Circuit expanded into multiple Monster Jam touring series with additional drivers, proving that the truck has become a successful new part of the Monster Jam lineup.

Photo by Charley Gallay/Getty Images

BIGFOOT

BIGFOOT is widely regarded as the original monster truck and one of the most influential vehicles in motorsports history. Created by Bob Chandler in the mid-1970s, BIGFOOT began as a heavily modified 1974 Ford F-250 pickup truck. Chandler, an off-road enthusiast from Missouri, initially customized the truck to promote his four-wheel-drive business, gradually adding larger tires, stronger suspension, and specialized drivetrain components to handle extreme conditions.

By 1979, the truck had evolved so dramatically that it is now officially recognized as the first monster truck, marking the birth of an entirely new form of motorsport. The name "BIGFOOT" reportedly came from Chandler's heavy driving style, which often caused mechanical breakages. What began as a promotional tool quickly captured public attention due to its size, power, and spectacle.

Firestone
FORD
ZF

One of the most important moments in BIGFOOT's history came in 1981, when Chandler filmed the truck crushing two junk cars as a demonstration. This stunt, initially intended as a joke, became a pre-social media sensation, and led to the first public car-crushing event shortly afterward. The act of crushing cars soon became the defining feature of monster truck shows and helped propel BIGFOOT to national fame.

Throughout the early 1980s, BIGFOOT dominated exhibitions and competitions, often outperforming rivals and drawing large crowds. As its popularity grew, other builders began creating similar oversized trucks, giving rise to the monster truck industry. Promoters started organizing events specifically for these vehicles, eventually leading to structured competitions and racing formats.

BIGFOOT also played a key role in shaping the sport's safety and organization. In 1987, Chandler helped establish the Monster Truck Racing Association, which introduced standardized rules and safety guidelines that are still influential today. Over time, multiple versions of BIGFOOT were built, each pushing technological boundaries with larger tires, stronger engines, and more advanced suspension systems. One version, BIGFOOT 5, even earned recognition as the largest monster truck ever, equipped with massive 10-foot-tall tires!

Beyond competition, BIGFOOT became a cultural icon, appearing in films, television, and live events across the United States and around the planet. Its legacy extends far beyond a single vehicle—it represents the origin of a global entertainment phenomenon. Today, monster truck shows continue to attract millions of fans worldwide and BIGFOOT, the "Sasquatch Sensation," has forever left its footprint as a symbol of innovation and spectacle.

Firestone
BIGFOOT
Firestone
HEDMAN HEDDERS
TRAXXAS
BOS Racing

THE DRI

ERS

GRAVE DIGGER
RIP
DENNIS ANDERSON
TO THY LEGION CRY
THOU SHALL ARISE
OF FLAMES AND THUNDER
TO CLAIM THY PRIZE
Kill Devil Hill
MONSTER JAM
SIMPSON
GRAVE DIGGER

ADAM ANDERSON

Adam Anderson (born December 5, 1985, in Norfolk, Virginia) is famous for piloting the iconic Grave Digger truck on the Monster Jam circuit. The son of legendary driver Dennis Anderson, creator of Grave Digger, Adam grew up immersed in the world of monster trucks, traveling with his father and learning the mechanics and performance side of the sport from an early age.

Anderson began his professional driving career in 2005, first competing in a truck called Vette King before moving into his own signature vehicle, Taz, which helped establish his reputation as a fearless and creative driver. His breakout moment came in 2008, when he won the Monster Jam World Finals Freestyle Championship at just 22 years old, becoming the youngest champion in that event's history.

Over the years, Anderson has driven several versions of Grave Digger, including Grave Digger the Legend, a tribute to his father's early truck design. He has built an impressive résumé, earning five Monster Jam World Championships, including three in racing (2013, 2014, 2018) and two in freestyle (2008, 2016). His ability to combine speed, control, and high-risk freestyle tricks has made him one of the most respected competitors in the sport.

Adam is part of a prominent monster truck family, with siblings like Ryan Anderson and Krysten Anderson, and the family is widely credited with helping shape modern monster truck culture.

Known for his aggressive driving style and showmanship, Adam continues to be a central figure in Monster Jam, carrying on his father's legacy while building one of his own.

20
26
THE DRIVERS
MONSTER TRUCKS
MADNESS AND BADNESS
MONSTER JAM
SIMPSON
Son-uva Digger

RYAN ANDERSON

Ryan Anderson is one of the most recognizable stars in Monster Jam. Born on November 16, 1989, in Norfolk, Virginia, Anderson comes from a legendary motorsports family. He is the son of Dennis Anderson, the creator of the iconic Grave Digger truck, and grew up immersed in the world of monster trucks alongside his siblings, including fellow driver and brother, Adam Anderson.

Anderson began his professional career in 2010, debuting behind the wheel of Monster Mutt and quickly making an impact by winning the Monster Jam Rookie of the Year award. His aggressive, high-energy driving style and willingness to attempt bold tricks set him apart early on. In 2011, he introduced his signature truck, Son-Uva Digger, a spin-off of his father's famous Grave Digger, and has driven it as his primary vehicle ever since.

Over the years, Anderson has built an impressive résumé, becoming a multiple-time Monster Jam World Champion. His major accomplishments include winning the World Finals Racing Championship in 2017 and the Freestyle Championship in 2018, along with several High Jump championships in the 2020s. Known for pushing the limits of what monster trucks can do, he also set a world record in 2020 for the longest bicycle (side wheelie) in a monster truck!

Beyond his competitive success, Anderson is widely admired for his "technically out of control" driving style, which blends precision with chaos to thrill audiences. His performances often feature daring backflips, saves, and freestyle runs that energize crowds and helped redefine the sport.

Today, Ryan continues to compete at the highest level of Monster Jam, carrying on his family's legacy while carving out his own identity as one of the sport's most innovative and exciting drivers.

KRYSTEN ANDERSON

Krysten Anderson, a member of the famous Anderson clan, has also taken her turn at the wheel of Grave Digger. Born on May 16, 1997, in Currituck, North Carolina, she grew up immersed in the world of motorsports as the daughter of legendary driver and Grave Digger creator Dennis Anderson. Surrounded by trucks and racing culture from infancy, Anderson developed a natural passion for the sport and eventually followed in her family's footsteps.

Anderson officially began her professional career in 2017, becoming the first full-time female driver for Team Grave Digger. Her debut season showcased her determination and adaptability, highlighted by winning a freestyle competition in only her second event. Despite the pressure of carrying one of the most famous names in monster truck history, she quickly established herself as a competitive and fearless driver.

Over the years, Anderson has built an impressive résumé of accomplishments. In 2020, she set a Guinness World Record for the highest ramp jump by a monster truck, reaching 33 feet 9.6 inches. Two years later, she made history again by becoming the first female Monster Jam series champion, winning the 2022 Arena Series Central title. That same year, she earned the Rising Star Award, further cementing her status as one of the sport's top talents.

Known for her families' iconic aggressive driving style and signature confidence, Anderson continues to compete at a high level while inspiring a new generation of female motorsports drivers. Her career represents both the continuation of a legendary family legacy and the evolution of monster truck racing into a more inclusive and diverse sport.

"THE LOUDEST, FASTEST ROLLER COASTER YOU'VE EVER BEEN ON."
— KRYSTEN ANDERSON

20
26
THE DRIVERS
MONSTER TRUCKS
MADNESS AND RADNESS
SIMPSON
GRAVE
DIGGER
MONSTER
JAM
EVENT
CHAMPIO

TYLER MENNINGA

Tyler Menninga is another driver who rose to fame while descending into the dirt piloting the iconic truck Grave Digger. Born in Minnesota, Menninga grew up immersed in motorsports culture, developing mechanical skills and a passion for high-performance vehicles at a young age. Before stepping into the driver's seat, he worked as part of the Grave Digger team, gaining hands-on experience preparing and maintaining the trucks, which helped him understand the intricacies of the brutish vehicles.

Menninga made his competitive debut in Monster Jam in 2016 and quickly rose through the ranks due to his precision driving style, consistency, and composure under pressure. Despite being relatively new to driving, he established himself as a dominant force in the sport. Known for his technical control in racing and freestyle events, Menninga has earned multiple Monster Jam World Championship titles, particularly excelling in the Racing Championship category.

Driving Grave Digger, one of the most legendary trucks in the sport, comes with high expectations, but Menninga has embraced the responsibility and legacy associated with it. His performances often blend speed with calculated risk, allowing him to execute clean runs while still thrilling audiences with big-air stunts and creative freestyle routines.

Off the track, Menninga is respected for his professionalism and dedication to the sport. He frequently engages with fans and represents Monster Jam as an ambassador of motorsports entertainment. His rapid success and continued dominance have solidified his reputation as one of the top drivers of his generation, and he remains a key figure in the evolving landscape of monster truck competition.

"I GREW UP WATCHING MONSTER JAM AND MONSTER TRUCKS, BUT I NEVER THOUGHT THAT I WOULD EVER BE BEHIND THE WHEEL OF GRAVE DIGGER."
— DRIVER TYLER MENNINGA

SOLDIER
FORTUNE
BLACK OPS
MONSTER JAM
SIMPSON

TONY OCHS

Tony Ochs is a highly respected driver, appreciated for his precision behind the wheel and long-standing dedication to the sport. With decades of experience, Ochs has built a reputation as both a skilled competitor and a reliable team member within the tight-knit monster truck community.

Ochs is applauded for his work as a driver for the iconic BIGFOOT Monster Trucks team, one of the most influential organizations in the history of monster trucking. BIGFOOT is widely credited with pioneering the sport, and being chosen as one of its drivers speaks to Ochs's talent and professionalism. During his time with the team, he has driven multiple versions of the BIGFOOT truck, performing in exhibitions, competitions, and live events across the United States.

Known for his smooth driving style and technical control, Ochs excels in freestyle and racing formats alike. His performances often emphasize consistency and vehicle preservation, qualities that are highly valued in a sport where mechanical strain is constant. Fans appreciate his ability to deliver exciting shows while maintaining a high level of safety and discipline.

Beyond competition, Ochs has also contributed to the sport through mentorship and public engagement. He frequently interacts with fans at events, helping to grow interest in monster trucks among younger audiences. His approachable personality and willingness to share insights about the sport have made him a popular figure off the track.

Throughout his career, Tony has exemplified the professionalism and passion that define monster truck driving. While not the most flamboyant driver, his cool demeanor and technical expertise have earned him lasting respect in an industry built on power, performance, and showmanship.

TONY OCHS CREDITS HIS 10-YEAR ARMY CAREER AS A US ARMY APACHE CREW CHIEF FOR HIS ABILITY TO HANDLE HIGH-STRESS SITUATIONS. WHEN DRIVING A MONSTER TRUCK, "YOU DON'T HAVE TIME TO BE SCARED," HE SAID.

BRIANNA MAHON

Brianna Mahon is a rising star, known for her skill, determination, and passion for motorsports. Growing up in a family deeply rooted in the monster truck industry, she was introduced to the sport at an early age. Her father, veteran driver Scott Hartsock, played a key role in inspiring her interest and guiding her development behind the wheel. Surrounded by engines, tools, and the roar of massive trucks, Mahon quickly developed both mechanical knowledge and driving confidence.

Mahon made her professional debut driving the monster truck Scooby-Doo, where she impressed fans with her control, consistency, and fearless approach to competition. Transitioning later to other trucks, including the iconic Wonder Woman in the Monster Jam circuit, she continued to build her reputation as a versatile and competitive driver. Her performances often highlight her ability to balance technical precision with crowd-pleasing stunts, making her a fan favorite at events across the country.

Beyond her driving skills, Mahon is also recognized as an important figure representing women in a traditionally male-dominated sport. She has become a role model for young fans, especially girls who aspire to enter motorsports. Through meet-and-greet events, social media, and public appearances, she actively encourages others to pursue their passions regardless of barriers.

Brianna's career reflects both her dedication to the sport and her willingness to push boundaries. As she continues to compete and evolve as a driver, she remains focused on improving her performance and leaving her own personal stamp on the monster truck community.

"THE FIRST TIME I GOT IN A TRUCK, I FELL IN LOVE. IT WAS A DREAM I NEVER KNEW I HAD." — BRIANNA MAHON

JESTER
MONSTER TRUCK
LUCAS OIL
JCB

MATT PAGLIARULO

Matt Pagliarulo is a longtime driver and team owner who found fame competing in major stadium monster truck series under his independent outfit, Tomfoolery Motorsports. He is based out of Sanford, Florida, and has built a family-centered racing program that includes multiple drivers from his household.

Pagliarulo's professional driving career began in 2015 when he debuted his signature truck, Jester, after previously working around the sport as a fan and crew member. His entry into driving was gradual—he spent time learning team operations and mechanics before committing to building and competing with his own truck.

One of his most notable career milestones came in 2017 when he competed in the Double Down Showdown event and earned the Rising Star of the Year recognition, signaling his emergence as a competitive independent driver on the national stage.

By 2020, Pagliarulo achieved a major breakthrough by winning his first stadium freestyle and event championship in Tampa, marking his first major competitive title in the sport.

Over the following years, he expanded Tomfoolery Motorsports into a multi-truck operation featuring vehicles such as Kraken, Wreckreation, Michigan Ice Monster, Excaliber, Mullet, and Missfire while also fielding entries for his children Nick, Michael, and Brooke Pagliarulo, all of whom became competitive drivers in their own right.

Pagliarulo has also been a regular competitor in stadium tours, consistently finishing mid-pack in points but remaining a respected independent competitor known for versatility and durability across different truck designs and events. His driving style is often described as evolving and adaptable, reflecting his experience across racing, freestyle, and exhibition events.

Overall, Matt's career is defined not only by his competition results but by his role as a builder of an independent monster truck team and a key figure in a multi-driver family racing legacy within the sport.

"AS A DAD, I'M SUPER PROUD THAT HE'S WORKED UP TO THE POINT WHERE HE CAN DRIVE. NOW HE'S A LOT BETTER THAN ME SO HE MAKES ME DRIVE A LITTLE BIT HARDER."

— DRIVER MATT PAGLIARULO ON HIS SON, NICK

MONSTER JAM
STARR CREATIONS
EXCALIBER

MICHAEL PAGLIARULO

Michael Pagliarulo is part of the Pagliarulo racing dynasty, which includes his father Matt and brother Nick and sister Brooke, all active in the sport. Michael's career reflects a rapid rise from crew member to full-time driver, shaped heavily by hands-on experience within the family operation.

He made his early start working on and assisting with the team's trucks, including performing mechanical and crew duties before moving into competition driving. His official full-size Monster Jam debut came at age 18, when he drove the family's flagship truck, Jester, at Pensacola, Florida. That debut was especially notable because he competed directly against his brother Nick, marking an early example of the family rivalry that has become a defining feature of his career.

After his debut, Michael expanded his driving opportunities across multiple trucks within the team. He has driven entries such as Excaliber and Michigan Ice Monster, showcasing versatility across different chassis and body styles. In 2024, he also debuted the truck Freedom Flyer at the Freedom Factory event, further establishing himself as a multi-truck competitor within independent monster truck circuits.

A key strength of Michael's career has been his ability to develop quickly through video and driver simulation study and family mentorship. He is known for analyzing past events to refine his technique, a habit that has helped him adapt to the high-intensity demands of stadium and arena competition.

His career accomplishments include becoming a full-time competitive driver for Tomfoolery Motorsports, contributing to multiple truck debuts, and participating in independent tours and Monster Jam-related events. While still early in his professional journey, Michael is widely viewed as a budding star with tremendous potential in the monster truck industry.

NICK PAGLIARULO

Nick Pagliarulo "sunk" to prominence for piloting the iconic truck Kraken on the global Monster Jam circuit. With a driving style that blends precision, aggression, and crowd awareness, Pagliarulo has built a reputation as one of the sport's most entertaining and technically skilled competitors.

Pagliarulo's path into monster trucks reflects a deep-rooted passion for motorsports. Like many drivers in the field, he developed an early fascination with high-powered vehicles and live motorsport events, eventually working his way into the highly competitive Monster Jam series. Behind the wheel of Kraken, a truck themed after the legendary sea creature, he quickly stood out for his ability to combine big air tricks with controlled, consistent racing performances.

Over the years, Pagliarulo has competed in stadiums and arenas across the United States and internationally, thrilling fans with freestyle runs that often feature daring combinations of jumps, wheelies, and bicycle maneuvers. His performances are known not just for their intensity, but also for their creativity–an essential trait in a sport where freestyle scoring rewards originality as much as execution.

In addition to his driving skills, Pagliarulo is recognized for his connection with fans. He frequently participates in pit parties and fan engagement events, where he shares insights into the sport and inspires younger audiences interested in motorsports. This accessibility has helped him build a loyal following within the Monster Jam community.

As monster truck racing continues to evolve, Nick remains a key figure in pushing the limits of what these massive machines can do. His commitment to performance, entertainment, and fan interaction ensures his ongoing impact on the sport.

20 26
THE DRIVERS
MONSTER TRUCKS
MADNESS AND BADNESS
TOM MEENTS
MAX-D
TOM MEENTS
Advance Auto Parts
MONSTER JAM
MAX-D
DECADE OF
MAXIMUM DESTRUCTION
ENERGY SUSPENSION
UNIVERSAL TECHNICAL INSTITUTE
PRO MAG
DERALE PERFORMANCE
OPTIMA BATTERIES
THE ULTIMATE POWER SOURCE
HAWK
LUCAS OIL PRODUCTS INC.
Advance Auto

THOMAS WILLIAM MEENTS

Tom Meents (full name Thomas William Meents) is definitely on the Mount Rushmore of monster truck drivers. Born on July 10, 1967, in Paxton, Illinois, he built a legendary career spanning more than three decades, competing from 1993 until his retirement in 2024. He is often nicknamed "The Professor" and considered by many fans and peers as the "GOAT" of monster truck drivers due to his innovation, consistency, and championship success.

Meents began his career in mud racing in the late 1980s with vehicles like "Shake Me," where his aggressive driving style quickly gained attention. His transition into monster trucks came in 1993 when he began driving Monster Patrol for Paul Shafer. This move marked the start of his rise in prominence, as he quickly proved himself a standout competitor and began winning major events, including the USHRA U.S. Truck Fest in 1997.

His breakthrough into mainstream fame came in 1999-2000 when he drove Bulldozer and then Goldberg, a truck themed after professional wrestler Bill Goldberg. With Goldberg, Meents won the inaugural Monster Jam World Finals Racing Championship in 2000 and achieved a rare sweep in 2001 by winning both racing and freestyle titles at the World Finals. This established him as one of the sport's elite competitors and a consistent championship contender.

Meents continued to evolve the sport through new trucks and innovations, including Team Meents (2001-2002) and his most famous creation, Maximum Destruction (Max-D), which debuted in 2003. With Max-D, he became known for aggressive driving, high-risk freestyle stunts, and technical precision. Over his career, he won 14 Monster Jam World Finals Championships across racing, freestyle, and skills competitions.

Some of his most notable accomplishments include multiple World Finals racing titles (2000, 2001, 2002, 2009, 2011, 2012), freestyle championships (2001, 2002, 2004, 2006, 2013, 2022), and pioneering stunts such as the first attempted monster truck backflip and the first successful front flip in competition. He also claimed fame for signature driving techniques like high-speed donuts, two-wheel balancing, and roof walking during freestyle runs.

Beyond competition, Meents contributed to the sport's development by helping design trucks and mentoring younger drivers through Monster Jam University. His influence helped shape modern freestyle monster truck driving standards.

After announcing his retirement tour in 2023, Tom officially stepped away from competition in 2024 following a long and decorated career, leaving behind a legacy as one of the most successful, innovative, and recognizable figures in monster truck history.

GRAVE DIGGER
Victory Lane EXTREME FINISHES
WWW.GRAVEDIGGER.COM
MONSTER JAM
MONSTERJAM.COM
GRAVE DIGGER RACE TEAM
GRAVE DIGGER
30TH
ANNIVERSARY
BAD TO THE BONE
GRAVE DIGGER .COM
2000 FREESTYLE CHAMPION
2004 RACING CHAMPION
2006 RACING CHAMPION
SIMPSON
Auto Meter
LUCAS OIL PRODUCTS INC.

DENNIS MONTAGUE ANDERSON

Dennis Montague Anderson (born October 24, 1960) is revered as one of the most influential figures in monster truck history and is legendary as the creator, owner, and original driver of the iconic Grave Digger monster truck. Nicknamed "The Icon" and "The Father of Freestyle," Anderson helped define modern Monster Jam-style freestyle competition through his aggressive, high-risk driving and innovative approach to truck design and performance.

Anderson began his career in the early 1980s after working on a farm and experimenting with mud racing. In 1982, he built the first version of Grave Digger using a 1951 Ford pickup body, reportedly naming it after a rival driver's taunt that he would "dig a grave" with his old vehicle. What started as a mud bogging machine quickly evolved into a competitive monster truck, eventually becoming one of the most recognizable motorsport vehicles in the world.

Throughout the late 1980s and 1990s, Anderson competed across major U.S. monster truck circuits, including the USHRA (United States Hot Rod Association). He gained fame for his fearless driving style, often pushing the truck to its limits and frequently crashing in spectacular fashion. This aggressive approach earned him the nickname "One Run Anderson," reflecting his tendency to either win big or break the truck in a single run.

His career reached elite status in the 2000s when he became a multiple-time Monster Jam World Finals champion. Anderson captured four world titles in total: a freestyle championship in 2000, and racing championships in 2004, 2006, and 2010. These victories cemented Grave Digger as a dominant force and helped propel Monster Jam into a mainstream motorsport entertainment brand.

Beyond competition, Anderson is also credited with building the Grave Digger team into a multi-truck operation. As demand for appearances grew, he expanded the brand, allowing other drivers to compete under the Grave Digger name while maintaining its signature look and performance identity. This expansion helped establish one of the most successful franchises in monster truck history.

Anderson's influence also extends through his family. Several of his children including Adam, Ryan, Krysten, and Weston have become professional Monster Jam drivers, continuing the Grave Digger legacy across generations.

He retired from full-time competition in 2017 following injuries but remains an iconic figure in the sport and occasionally makes appearances in exhibition events. Today, Dennis is celebrated not only for his championships but for shaping monster truck freestyle driving into the high-energy, crowd-focused spectacle it is today.

TIRES

Monster truck tires are among the most extreme off-road tires in existence, engineered specifically to support the enormous size, weight, and performance demands of monster trucks used in competitions, exhibitions, and freestyle events. These tires are instantly recognizable due to their massive height, typically 66 inches tall, and their wide, heavily treaded design.

One of the defining features of monster truck tires is their construction. Most traditional monster truck tires are bias-ply tires rather than radial. Bias-ply construction uses multiple layers of rubber-coated nylon cords laid at alternating angles. This makes the tire extremely durable and resistant to punctures, which is critical when landing jumps or crushing vehicles. While radial tires offer better heat dissipation and smoother rides, bias-ply designs are preferred in many monster truck applications because they provide stronger sidewalls and more predictable deformation under extreme loads.

MEGALODON
MONSTER JAM
BKT
BKT
BKT
LOT
J
MERCHANDISE
OFFICIAL MERCHANDISE
2026
FEATURE
MONSTER TRUCKS
MADNESS AND BADNESS

The size of these tires is another standout characteristic. A single tire can weigh between 800 and 900 pounds depending on the model and manufacturer. Because of this weight, handling and mounting them requires specialized equipment and multiple crew members. The rims are also unusually large, typically around 25 inches in diameter, and are beadlock wheels that mechanically clamp the tire in place to prevent it from slipping off during low-pressure use or high-impact maneuvers.

Monster truck tires operate at very low air pressures, often between 8 and 10 psi, which allows for maximum surface contact and shock absorption. This low pressure helps the tire flex significantly, improving traction and cushioning landings from jumps that can exceed 30 feet in the air. The large voids and deep lugs in the tread pattern are designed for extra grip on dirt, mud, crushed cars, and arena surfaces, rather than for road use.

Common manufacturers of monster truck tires include companies like Goodyear, Firestone, and specialty off-road tire builders who produce custom designs for racing teams and events. The tires are typically repurposed from agricultural or military applications and heavily modified to meet the demands of monster truck performance.

Overall, monster truck tires are a crucial component of the sport, combining brute strength, engineered flexibility, and massive scale to withstand some of the most extreme conditions in motorsports.

BKT
BKT

SUSPENSI

Monster truck suspensions are engineered to handle extreme loads, massive impacts, and highly variable terrain, making them very different from typical automotive suspension systems. A modern monster truck can weigh around 10,000 - 12,000 pounds and run tires that are over five feet tall, so the suspension must absorb enormous forces while maintaining control and durability during jumps, crashes, and high-speed runs.

At the core of most monster truck suspension systems is a four-link solid axle setup, combined with either coil-over shocks or, more commonly in competition trucks, large nitrogen-charged shock absorbers. These shocks are often custom-built and can be more than 2 - 3 inches in diameter, with multiple internal stages to manage different levels of compression. The four-link design connects the axle to the truck's frame using four rigid control arms, which keep the axle properly positioned while still allowing vertical movement.

ON

One of the most distinctive features of monster truck suspension is its massive travel range. While a typical off-road vehicle might have 10 - 20 inches of suspension travel, a monster truck can have 26 - 36 inches or more! This allows the truck to land from heights of 30 feet or greater without immediately wrecking its chassis or driver. The shock absorbers are carefully tuned with internal valving systems that control how quickly the suspension compresses and rebounds, preventing the truck from bouncing uncontrollably after a landing.

Air pressure and nitrogen gas play a major role in shock performance. The nitrogen is used to prevent foaming in the hydraulic fluid during repeated high-impact landings, which helps maintain consistent damping performance. Many systems also use remote reservoirs attached to the shocks, increasing fluid capacity and heat dissipation during continuous runs.

Another key component is adjustability. Teams can fine-tune ride height, rebound speed, and compression stiffness depending on the event and track conditions. For example, an indoor racing course with tight turns may require stiffer settings for stability, while an outdoor freestyle event prioritizes softer suspension for bigger jumps and longer airtime.

Durability is also critical. Monster truck suspension components are made from high-strength steel alloys and are often overbuilt to survive repeated catastrophic loads. Despite this, components still wear out quickly and are frequently rebuilt or even replaced between events.

Overall, monster truck suspensions are a blend of heavy-duty engineering and precise tuning, designed to balance chaos and control in one of motorsport's most extreme environments.

BKT

MERCH

Monster truck merchandise, especially branded around major series like Monster Jam, has grown into a surprisingly large and culturally sticky part of the monster truck world. What began as simple t-shirts and diecast toy trucks has expanded into a full-scale lifestyle merch ecosystem that mirrors the sport's evolution from niche motorsport spectacle to mainstream family entertainment.

At the center of this collectible culture are licensed toy trucks, often produced in partnership with major companies like Hot Wheels in earlier years and currently Spin Master. These diecast models replicate famous trucks such as Grave Digger, Max-D, Megalodon, and others, often in multiple scales (1:64, 1:24, and larger collector editions). The toys are usually released in series, chase variants, and special editions tied to events or anniversaries, which encourages collecting. Over time, fans don't just buy one truck–they try to complete entire lineups, which drives repeat purchases and secondary market activity.

Photo by Joe Funk

Beyond toys, monster truck merch includes apparel (hoodies, hats, jerseys), novelty items like light-up cups, flags, pit-party collectibles, and event-exclusive souvenirs. At live events, merch booths are a major attraction; families often spend a large chunk of their experience budget there, reinforcing the idea that merch is part of the "show," not just an add-on. Some fans also love that exclusive items only available at specific events amps up desirability.

Popularity-wise, monster truck merch thrives because it connects multiple audiences at once. Children are drawn to the bright colors, oversized designs, and toy-like branding of trucks, while adults often engage through nostalgia or collecting. Modern monster truck design has even leaned into a "giant toy" aesthetic, by designing new trucks and color schemes that will look great as models and on shirts, which strengthens the feedback loop between live shows and merchandise consumption.

Collectibility is a major driver of long-term engagement. Limited releases, retired truck designs, and "special edition" paint schemes can become highly sought after. Some collectors focus on specific teams or drivers, while others aim for complete historical sets. Condition, packaging, and rarity all affect resale value, with unopened diecast trucks often trading at a premium in online marketplaces.

Overall, monster truck merch has become more than souvenirs—it functions as a collectible ecosystem that extends the excitement of live events into everyday life. Its popularity persists because it blends spectacle, nostalgia, and structured collecting in a way that appeals across generations.

Photo by Joe Funk

LUCAS OIL PRODUCTS INC.
LUCAS OIL
IT WORKS!